THE
TEXAS
ARCHIVE WAR

THE
TEXAS
ARCHIVE WAR

HOUSTON AND LAMAR BATTLE FOR THE CAPITAL

LORA-MARIE BERNARD

FOREWORD BY LINDSAY SCOVIL

THE
History
PRESS

Published by The History Press
Charleston, SC
www.historypress.com

First published 2024

Manufactured in the United States

ISBN 9781467156059

Library of Congress Control Number: 2023949142

For everyone who knows that Texas is more than its political theater,
but they can't walk away from the show.

"March, Chieftain, to the Battle Fly"

March, Chieftain, to the battle fly
And wear thy falcon on thy thigh
To meet a ruthless enemy
And strike for victory!

The day will come when it shall be
Thy fate to meet the enemy
And see the base invader flee
From Anglo-Saxon chivalry.

This armor on thy person placed
Was made to shield a warrior's breast
Who guards the weak that are oppressed,
His due from chivalry!

When in the battle van you move
Thy thoughts in other scenes may rove
Nor meet a corresponding love
Of her who arms thee now.

But still the heart must e'er admire
The deeds that flash from valor's fire
To blast the base invader's ire.
Such deeds shall be adorned.

Adieu! Nor cease the hero's toil
While foes pollute our sacred soil
Go, mingle in the deathly broil
And make a nation free!

Lady, thy mandate I'll obey
And make it good in mortal fray
Or ne'er survive the battle day
To greet thy smile again.

Should I return from well-fought fields
I'll bring again thy warrior's shield
And at thy feet I'll proudly yield
The laurels won for thee.

—To Anna Raquet, from Sam Houston
Columbia, New Year's Day 1837

CONTENTS

FOREWORD

By Lindsay Scovil

executive director, Lake Jackson Historical Association
executive director and editor, Houston History Alliance,
Handbook of Houston (2015-19)

In the annals of history, wars are often recognized by the thunderous roar of cannons, the clash of armies on distant battlefields and the decisive moments that reshape the course of nations. Yet the most profound and intriguing wars are those that unfold not on the fields of battle but within the corridors of power, where words become weapons and the fates of nations hang in the balance. The Archive War, an episode of Texas history that has been pushed into obscurity, is one such extraordinary saga.

In the pages that follow, Lora-Marie Bernard will take readers on a journey into the heart of the Texas Republic, a young and burgeoning nation struggling to define itself in the tumultuous aftermath of the Texas Revolution. This narrative offers a meticulous examination of a pivotal moment in Texas history when political feuds, rivalries and a difference of visions pushed the nascent republic to the brink of a civil war. It was a war fought not with muskets and long rifles but with ink, words and a fervent determination that resonated as loudly as any cannon.

The Archive War, as the reader shall come to understand, was no isolated skirmish; it was the culmination of a longstanding conflict between two prominent figures in Texas politics, Mirabeau Lamar and Sam Houston. As Lamar stood on the cusp of his inauguration as the second president of the Republic of Texas, the unexpected and audacious appearance of

Sam Houston, the retiring president, transformed what should have been a day of solemn political transition into dramatic pageantry that captured the collective imagination of the Texan people. In this clash of oratory and ideals, it became evident that Texas politics were not merely a matter of policy; they were a matter of charisma, identity and destiny.

Lamar's ascension to the presidency marked the beginning of a contentious era in Texan history. He envisioned a Texas that would stand as a sovereign nation, forging alliances with other world superpowers. His vehement opposition to annexation by the United States was at odds with Houston's vision for Texas's future. Houston, the consummate general, played his hand in the political arena with all the magnetism and hubris that had made him a legendary figure in Texan history.

The struggle between Houston and Lamar was not limited to the question of annexation; it extended into every facet of Texas policy. Their conflicting worldviews led them to vastly different ideological beliefs, despite sharing the same political space. Thus, the stage was set for a dramatic rivalry.

Lamar's bold decision to relocate the Texas capital from Houston to the site that would eventually become Austin epitomized the zeal of this political era. Yet it was not the end of the story. When Houston returned to the presidency, he ardently renewed his efforts to relocate the capital back to Houston. The Archive War, one of the most remarkable episodes in Texas history, stands as a testament to the lengths to which these two titans were willing to go to shape the future of their beloved Texas.

As we delve deeper into the narrative, we shall witness a war unlike any other. It was a war that brought to the forefront questions of governance, identity and sovereignty. It was a war that tested the limits of political power and the resilience of a young republic.

In recounting the Archive War, Lora-Marie Bernard does more than simply resurrect a forgotten chapter of Texas history; she sheds light on the intricate history of a nation's formation and development, guiding us to examine the conflicting aspects of leadership, where charm and political skill often clash.

As we embark on this journey through the turbulent days of the Archive War, we as readers are invited to ponder the profound impact of personalities, policies and pivotal moments in the making of history. Perhaps this examination of the Archive War will illuminate not only the events of that time but also the enduring human struggle for self-determination and the pursuit of a vision—however divergent it may be—for a better future.

ACKNOWLEDGEMENTS

I'd like to thank Ben Gibson and the team at The History Press for their continuing belief in my ability to write books they want to publish.

To Michael Bailey, I acknowledge that I'd never want to do history without him.

The chapter "Houston on Display" would never have been written without James and Linley Glover and everyone they called on my behalf. Special thanks to Kay Gray, a collection manager at the Bryan Museum in Galveston, for her generous and kind help.

Lindsay Scovil's foreword is amazing, and I'm grateful she did it, but I really want to thank her for letting me join her squad.

Without question, I thank all the friends of Bobby Gervais for taking him anywhere they could think of so I could write this book.

Finally, there's Bobby Gervais. Just Bobby.

PART I
BATTLEFIELD WARS

1

GEORGE WASHINGTON

Mirabeau B. Lamar was at his inauguration as the second president of the Republic of Texas when the first president of the United States seemed to appear.

Lamar's inauguration occurred in 1838 inside the unpretentious capitol building in Houston, Texas.

"A great crowd had assembled to witness the inauguration of Lamar as the second President of the Republic," recalled W.Y. Allen during a recounting of his remembrances of Texas. "It was expected by his friends that his inaugural would be a politico-oratorical production, as he had the reputation of being a fine writer and poet."

That's not what happened.

Allen recalled Lamar's predecessor, President Sam Houston, strode past him as thousands in the audience cheered. The unannounced and unplanned move infuriated Lamar. He watched dumbfounded from the pew.

"Houston, knowing something of Lamar's nervousness, took occasion to make an exaugural," Allen recalled.

Houston had delighted the crowd, wrote William Caney Crane, the president of Baylor University in 1884.

> *The assembled multitude, in a burst of indignation, clamored for the hero of San Jacinto. He came forward to the front of the Capitol. A wild shout of enthusiasm rent the sky as the people gazed upon his lofty, ample, and heroic form, relieved against the portrait of George Washington, which was suspended behind him.*

Left: George Washington. *Author's collection; from the public domain.*

Right: Sam Houston. *Author's collection; from the public domain.*

Opposite: Mirabeau Lamar. *Courtesy of the Texas State Library and Archives Commission.*

Within minutes, Houston had successfully hijacked Lamar's inauguration. Over the centuries, that scene would be rewritten as if Houston himself had dressed like Washington, a testament to Houston's oracle power.

"For three hours he held the thousands before him under the force of his impetuous eloquence," Crane wrote. "The scroll of the history of Texas was unrolled, her future policy was portrayed; her future destiny, if a sound policy was pursued, was set forth in prophetic speech."

The power of this rhetoric may have been the result of refreshing alcoholic drinks.

William Ransom Hogan noted in his 1942 dissertation, "The generation that maintained Texas as a republic drank heavily and frequently. Enormous amounts of intoxicants were imbibed in the boom towns, chief among which was Houston."

Houston might have just been drunk, or it could have been the power of his own words that overwhelmed him.

"The tears streamed down his face as, in conclusion, he took farewell of the people he loved," Cane wrote. "Extending his broad arms over the

MIRABEAU B. LAMAR.

people, he poured out, from his great heart, the benediction of a true patriot and invincible soldier. The vast multitude responded with tears to his tears."

By the time a bawling Houston walked away, no one wanted to hear Lamar's vision for a new kind of republic.

The crowd wanted more of Houston's vision and had no problems letting it be known, according to Crane.

"The still deep murmur of subdued feeling closed the excitement of the solemnly moving scene," he wrote.

Even Lamar, who seethed as Houston enraptured the audience didn't want to be there. He left.

"Lamar had become so nervous that he could not read his inaugural, and had to commit it to his private secretary, Algernon Thompson, to be read to an exhausted audience," Allen recollected.

Houston's theatrical spectacle was juxtaposed by Lamar's grounded words steeped in policy and clear-eyed vision.

Lamar's speech made it clear he was going to crush every accomplishment Houston extolled to the crowd that day.

Most of Lamar's speech was designed to ridicule Houston's vision to annex Texas into the United States. Lamar envisioned a Texas Empire. He dreamed the republic would become economic allies with Great Britain and Europe.

> *I have never been able myself to perceive the policy of the desired connexion [sic], or discover in it any advantage either civil, political, or commercial which could possibly result to Texas. [Annexation]…the step once taken would produce a lasting regret, and ultimately prove as disastrous to our liberty and hopes, as the triumphant sword of the enemy. And I say this from no irreverence to the character and institutions of my native country, whose welfare I have ever desired, and do still desire above my individual happiness.*

Thomas's delivery of Lamar's words fell flat. Houston had enthralled the crowd in an ad-libbed soliloquy of Texas's great qualities. None of them wanted to consider any idea of a nation that competed with countries on a global scale.

"Instead of vesting hopes in annexation or treaties, he implored the people to rely on their own public and private virtue and be magnanimous and just with all men and all nations," Crane wrote.

Texans elected Lamar as president after one of the most bizarre campaigns in history. He was overwhelmingly elected.

After the election, Crane wrote that some Texans thought Houston-mania might wane. They were wrong. Instead, Texas politics became more heated as Lamar and Houston each poured fuel on their feud.

"A vast concourse, larger than ever had been assembled before in Texas, gathered to witness the closing scenes of [Houston's] administration and the inauguration of a new President," he wrote.

After the Texas Revolution ended, battles moved from the field to the legislative chambers. The men played strategic games that they strained to outmaneuver for the rest of their lives. Houston battled with his charm, personality and brash candor. Lamar battled with his intellect and heroics.

Annexation was only one of many policy battles that the two statesmen had wrangled. They agreed on nothing.

In fact, the men may have worked in the same capitol buildings, but they lived in entirely different republics.

As Houston's vice-president, Lamar was a constant antagonist. He rallied an anti-Houston coalition during the general's administration that created chaos at the capital.

Perhaps Houston believed he deserved to deliver a three-hour farewell address. He deserved to show he was an inspired statesman touched by the hand of God or, at least, George Washington.

Crane wrote that Houston was indeed that. The inaugural hijacking was proof of Houston's ability to whip up the troops, citizens and audience into a patriotic frenzy of public approval whenever he desired.

"Houston had demonstrated all the qualities of soldier, statesman, and orator, and in each character had placed his name on the rolls of immortality," Cane wrote.

In the end, why Houston made a scene didn't matter. Houston had found a good enemy in Lamar. Lamar had found a good enemy in the first president of the Republic of Texas.

The rematch game was on. Texas politics had become the new battlefield and policies had become weapons.

Over the course of three administrations, Texas swung back and forth on more than its nationhood. The relationships with the Native Americans and

Mexico were difficult to settle. Western expansion had become risky and difficult to conduct.

The high-stakes policies that floated between Lamar and Houston became the foundation of Texas political theater as we know it today.

Before Lamar's term ended, he refused to govern the new nation in a city named after his predecessor. It had taken him a matter of weeks to move the capital of Texas from Houston City to the "site of the town of Waterloo, on the north bank of the Colorado."

Today, that site is known as the city of Austin.

Years later, Houston regained the presidency for the last time. It took him only months to start a covert operation to bring the capital back to Houston City.

As great and wild as Texas political theater ever was, the Texas Archive Wars was the only time it involved a cannon, a vigilante committee, a manhunt and the theft of national papers.

2

THE DANGEROUS MISSION

The man who brought Lamar and Houston together was James Fannin, who, by his own admission, had been looking for something dangerous.

December 1835 was the dawning of the Texas Revolution against Mexico. It would be only a few months before the Mexican government would begin a bloody siege that would test the U.S. settlers who wanted to take a piece of Mexico for their own.

Captain Fannin, a Georgian, learned that Houston, the major general of the Texian army, had desired to promote him to colonel. Fannin wasn't happy because he had thought the position wasn't dangerous enough. It did not capture his fancy.

Given Fannin's huffiness about the offer, Houston gave him command of a reconnaissance mission for a big military gamble called the Matamoros Campaign.

That campaign focused on the capture of the rich and prosperous Matamoros Port. Some of those who supported the campaign had calculated Texas could gain as much as $100,000 a month if the army could gain control of it. Once the new republic was founded, that figure would have been more than enough to keep cash flowing to build a new nation.

After Fannin had taken charge, he quickly learned he managed an unruly band of soldiers who never wanted to take orders. The ego-driven, obstinate and unskilled troops were a persistent problem that Houston had also faced.

Nonetheless, Fannin led the battalion as he had been ordered. Along the way, he even organized relief missions when he learned about undermanned troops that faced the Mexicans.

James Fannin. *Courtesy of the Texas State Library and Archives Commission.*

FANNIN'S FRIEND FROM GEORGIA

Lamar, a fellow Georgian, was so impressed with Fannin that he closed shop in Georgia and moved to the Mexican Territory in 1835. He had plans to buy land and become a Texian.

He had money from his brother to support him. He had dreams to write about the territory that had captured his imagination. He wrote and gathered much of the region's history, but first, he became a rebel like Fannin.

The Alamo. *Courtesy of the Library of Congress.*

Lamar was among those who refortified and rebuilt Fort Velasco, a Mexican post that the townsfolk had taken in 1832. It was on the mouth of the Brazos River in Brazoria County.

During this time, Lamar, a prolific poet, submitted three poems to the *Brazoria Texas Republican.* Meanwhile, Fannin continued to execute his dangerous mission.

Fannin sailed his troops from Velasco to Copano. There, he gathered four companies of the Georgia Battalion, many of whom Lamar knew.

Fannin and his troops had planned to go to Refugio to help the troops there when they learned Mexican troops had landed in Matamoros. That caused Fannin to withdraw to Goliad, twenty-five miles north.

In Goliad, he and the troops waited while Mexican forces continued a successful advance into Texian territory.

General Santa Anna had led the siege under the principle of one law he'd pushed through the government. The law basically said any rebel was a traitor who should be caught and shot. He did not always follow it though. On occasion, he released prisoners captured during the siege.

In February 1836, Santa Anna's troops swelled near Bexar. This caused revolutionary William B. Travis to write a passionate letter to Houston asking for help at the Alamo, a small mission he commanded.

"Do hasten on to and me as rapidly as possible, or from the superior numbers of the enemy, it will be impossible for us to keep them out much longer," Travis wrote. "If they overpower us, we fall a sacrifice at the shrine of our country, and we hope posterity and our country will our memory justice. Give me help, oh my country.—Victory or death."

Fannin had attempted to reach the Alamo to help Travis, but his overweighted wagons and equipment became stuck in the San Antonio River. This meant the troops had to stop to let the animals rest. That night, the oxen wandered off.

As the troops dealt with their predicament, the Alamo fell weeks later on March 6, 1836, and the bodies of Travis and his troops were burned in a mass grave. About a week later, as Houston tried to control untrained troops in Gonzalez, he heard about the Alamo.

He sent word for Fannin to retreat, but Fannin did not.

Decisions at Goliad

Fannin instead continued to send troops to help those facing the Mexican siege, and once they needed help, he'd send more troops to assist them.

In need of supplies, Fannin retreated to Presidio La Bahia, the formidable fort in Goliad where he told troops to destroy anything they couldn't carry. When they left, they carried nine cannons and more than five hundred muskets.

The massive haul was a fatal decision.

The supplies were once again too much for the animals. After a mere six miles, Fannin ordered the troops to stop so the oxen could rest. Hours later, the Mexican cavalry appeared, and a fierce battle ensued. The next day, Fannin surrendered at the Battle of Coleto.

Fannin believed that his troop's lives would be spared. General Jose Urrea leaned toward the same thought. The Mexican commander made an appeal to Santa Anna, but he rebuffed Urrea.

Less than ten days later, on March 27, 1836, Santa Anna ordered Fannin and his troops to die in a massacre. The Mexican troops killed hundreds of men, including the Georgia Battalion, in front of Fannin. Then they

La Bahia, where James Fannin and his troops gathered supplies. *Courtesy of the Library of Congress.*

blindfolded him and shot him in the face. Their bodies, like those at the Alamo, were burned in a mass grave.

The incident reverberated a fear and concern throughout the United States. Rumors swirled about the troops' bloody fate at Goliad. With the demise of the Alamo, the United States wanted to believe Fannin would become the avenger.

For months after the massacre, the leaders of the United States tried to wrap their minds around what transpired. A March 28 report received in New York and printed on April 29 in the *Newburyport Herald* summed up the national sentiment:

> *As all rumors tend that way, it is probably that Goliad has fallen, but whether the garrison of 450 men have been slaughtered like that of the Alamo, or whether they had abandoned it before the approach of the Mexicans, cannot at present be ascertained.*
>
> *One account says they surrendered prisoners of war, and were afterwards massacred, but this must be a false rumor. As at the last advices, Col. Fanning [sic] and his garrison manifested an intention to stand by their position to the last; and this is described on all hands to be a very strong fort, by many deemed impregnable, it is quite possible that nearly the whole*

garrison may have fallen. It should be borne in mind, however, that we have no authentic accounts of the capture of Goliad.

The public was stunned. The fort was strong, and Fannin had a reputation as a brave fighter.

In fact, on April 14, the *Nashville Banner* still reported that it believed Fannin was ready to fight a winning battle inside the fort.

The *Newburyport Herald* editors agreed.

"Heavy firing was heard in that direction on the 14th [at Goliad] and no doubt was entertained that a desperate attack was then being made on the fort. Fannin and his men continued up to the latest dates to be in high spirits—even after the fall of San Antonio," read a report reprinted in the April 29 edition of the *Newburyport Herald*.

But in the same edition, a report that came in after the initial one confirmed the deaths of the troops and made clear the bloody siege was firmly underway.

"We have just received the copy of a letter from Brazoria, under the date March 24, which speaks of 'all settlements situated between the river Mueces [*sic*] and Los Brazos [San Felipe de Austin included] as overrun by the Mexican troops, who gave no quarter to those taken in their hands,'" the unsigned report stated.

(The report also mentioned that Santa Anna had emancipated the enslaved people in Texas.)

In time, newspapers began to criticize Houston's maneuvers. They questioned if his constant retreats were "necessary or convenient."

They blamed Houston for Fannin's death because he had ordered a retreat, which they believed Fannin had been trying to follow. Anonymous reports from Texas speculated on Fannin's death.

Instead of remaining in that Fort, where they might have maintained themselves, or at the worst would have sold their lives at a heavy expense to the Mexicans, they abandoned and blew up the Fort (thus giving a signal to the enemy in case they should be near,) and attempted to effect a junction with General Houston on the Colorado. They had scarcely marched six miles from the Fort when they were overtaken and surrounded by the Mexican cavalry and probably all cut to pieces, except a small advance guard, which escaped. It should however be stated in justification of Major Fanning [sic] that in abandoning and blowing up the Fort he acted in obedience to the positive orders of Gen. Houston.

Lamar Becomes an Avenger

Felix Huston, a Texian army member, was another who opined in the newspapers what Fannin's massacre would mean to the independence effort.

"If Col. Fannin has been defeated, the Texans have lost on the frontier about 600 men, and gained a month's delay," he wrote in the *Natchez Daily Courier.* His account was printed in many U.S. newspapers a few weeks later.

Lamar was devastated when he heard about the horror of the Goliad Massacre. The battalion was filled with Georgian friends, including Fannin.

That moment framed Lamar's opinion of Santa Anna and the Mexican army. The general was a liar and guilty of war crimes. Years later, Lamar still felt the sting.

> *Under any point of view whatsoever the shooting of Fannin and his companions, after celebrating a treaty with them in which their lives were granted them, was nothing less than perfidy and assassination two crimes of the greatest atrocity that could neither be excused nor pardoned simply because they were committed to please a corrupt government, or because it was necessary to promote the aggrandizement of an ambitious man.*

When he heard about the fate of his friends, Lamar wanted to know where to enlist.

The townspeople sent him to Harrisburg, where the rebel government leading the revolution had moved.

He walked there.

When he arrived, the leaders of the rebel government told him where to enlist. They sent him to San Felipe de Austin.

Before he left Harrisburg, Lamar wrote to his brother on April 10 that he was prepared to die.

> *I leave in the morning for the army: a dreadful Battle is to be fought in three or four days on the Brazos, decisive of the fate of Texas. I shall of course have to be in it....Houston's army has retreated from the Colorado to the Brazos: the Mexican army is in San Felipe, ours is 20 miles from them; they will come together in a few days, I shall reach Houston day after tomorrow, a distance from this place about 50 miles.*

With that, Lamar prepared himself to follow Houston, the man many blamed for the death of his friends.

3

THE CAPITAL OF LIFE

Remember this: I am forever Texas!
I keep the archives of her early years;
I was her citadel,—her outpost station;
I was the gateway of her pioneers."

—*Georgia Cummings Bader, Austin County poet,*
descendant of San Felipe de Austin pioneers

Majestic San Felipe de Austin stood on a prairie bluff near the Arroyo Dulce Creek, which ran into the west bank of the Brazos River.

It sat near the old Atascosita Trail. Its fertile and rich bottomlands stretched out for everyone to see.

Stephen F. Austin founded the town in 1824. He used it as the unofficial capital for the first Texas colony and his home base.

"Stephen F. Austin had established his headquarters something like half a mile back from the river on the west bank of a little creek—Palmito—that ran into the Brazos just above the main village," recalled Noah Smithwick, an early settler. "Just above Austin's house was the farm of Joshua Parker. Austin's house was a double log cabin with a wide 'passage' through the center, a porch with dirt floor on the front with windows opening upon it, and chimney at each end of the building."

San Felipe de Austin was a perfect new town, according to an emigrant who chronicled his experiences.

Left: Stephen F. Austin. *Courtesy of the Texas State Library and Archives Commission.*

Right: Noah Smithwick. *Author's collection; from the public domain.*

"The town is beautifully situated upon an elevated and fertile plain, admirably adapted for gardens and the cultivation of either trees or field crops," the emigrant wrote. "The country about it is beautiful, exhibiting, in close connection, elegant undulating prairies, rich level bottoms, and, in some directions, dense forest."

There were two ways to settle in San Felipe de Austin. Settlers could work directly with the Mexican government and contract their own pieces of property, or they could work with a land agent, known as an *empresario*. The empresario handled the issues with the government for them. Twenty-six empresarios worked in Texas. Austin was the most successful one.

"It was far better for the settler to be under the empresario system, because the difference of language and of race, as well as the red tape of the governmental procedure, often swamped the individual in his dealings with the government at Mexico City, or at Saltillo, and left him, after years of hard work and privations, without good title to the land he had developed," wrote Amelia Williams in her dissertation for the University of Texas in 1931.

"Moreover, the empresario had more power with the government than the ordinary man, and could attend to all the legalities for his entire colony

A replica depicting a San Felipe de Austin cabin before the town burned. *Courtesy of the San Felipe de Austin State Historic Site via Facebook.*

with far greater ease and expedition than the individual settler could for his single grant," she wrote.

San Felipe de Austin was eighty miles overland from the mouth of the river and two hundred miles by boat. Surveyor Seth Ingram planned the city using the Mexican model. It had four plazas, or villas. He built the streets and avenues on a grid, recalled resident Noah Smithwick.

By 1827, San Felipe was still a fledgling settlement, but it had grown substantially. Settlers constructed buildings to suit their lifestyles rather than impress anyone.

"In the absence of a more comprehensive view, a pen picture of the old town may not be interesting," Smithwick wrote. "The buildings all being of unhewn logs with clapboard roofs, presented few distinguishing features. Twenty-five or perhaps thirty log cabins strung along the west bank of the Brazos River was all there was of it, while the whole human population of all ages and colors could not have exceeded 200."

These two hundred settlers included ten Mexicans. More striking is that men outnumbered women two to one. Smithwick recalled that this led to many elaborate parties.

There being so little opportunity for social intercourse with the gentler sex, the sterner element should not be too severely censured if they sought diversion of a lower order, And [sic] if our stag parties were a bit convivial, they would probably compare favorably in that regard with the swell club dinners in the cities.

Godwin Cotton and Judge Williamson, known as "Three-Legged Willie," were usually the hosts. Cotton would coax Smithwick into helping the pair concoct competitions and feasts. A popular competition involved storytelling and dancing and was called a jag. "Thus while there was a scarcity of ladies of any kind in San Felipe, single ladies were indeed few and far between," Smithwick recalled. "Occasionally one ventured into town to be almost immediately captured by some aspirant for matrimonial honors."

Smithwick recalled Miss Eliza Picket married William C. White, Miss Westall married Brown Austin, Miss Jane Wilkins wed the alcalde Thomas Duke and Miss Scott became Mrs. Samuel May Williams.

Miss Pickett was the daughter of Mrs. Parmelia Pickett, a widow with money. She wed Jared E. Groce, who was called the richest man in the country and had a nearby plantation.

"The leadership of the 'ton' was accredited to Mrs. Jane Long, the widowed sister of Mrs. Alexander Calvet, and widow of General Long," Smithwick wrote.

VILLAS, SALOONS, CHURCHES AND SCHOOLS

Within the decade, the community sprawled westward from the river and reached inland. The "villas" had different functions, Smithwick recalled.

It must not be understood that these rows of buildings presented an unbroken or even regular line of front; every fellow built to suit himself, only taking care to give himself plenty of room, so that the town was strung along either side of the road something like half a mile.

John McFarland operated a ferry in the Commercial Plaza. Boats and wharfs loaded and unloaded there.

Two blocks south of McFarland's ferry was the Constitution Plaza, or "suburban villa," as Smithwick called it.

A saloon and billiard hall, Cooper and Chieves, came first for gambling and strong liquor. The liquor was available to "wash down the meals." The hall closed at 10:00 p.m.

"At San Felipe de Austin and Brazoria, leading villages in Austin's Colony, much of the gambling was centered around the game of billiards, which eventually became widely played in Texas towns," Williams wrote.

Smithwick recalled his home had been on the west bank of the river.

> *Going on down to the town proper, which lay along the west bank of the Brazos, the first house on the left was my bachelor abode, and near it, on the same side, stood the "village smithy" over which I presided.*

Gail Borden Jr. operated a blacksmith shop next door. Jonathan and Angelina Peyton owned the second tavern in town. Later, Angelina operated the local hotel.

> *Then came the Peyton tavern, operated by Jonthan C. Peyton and wife; the house was the regulation double log cabin. The saloon and billiard hall of Cooper and Chieves, the only frame building in the place, was next below the Peyton's [sic]. The first house on the right as you entered the town from above was Dinsmore's store, and next it the store of Walter C. White.*

William B. Travis operated a law office and acted as a local politician until he left for battle. J.H. Kuykendall helped him run the office.

Samuel May Williams operated the post office. He conducted the town business when Austin was away. Austin spent much of his time with Mexican officials in Mexico.

Thomas J. Pilgrim, a Baptist, had a proper "English school" with forty pupils, mostly boys. He also hosted the town's Sunday school, which he called a Sabbath school. A few years after he opened his school, three private schools began operating in the region. They advertised in the newspapers for new students, much to Pilgrim's chagrin.

One of these new schools boasted a student population of 424. Pilgrim was not shy in his assessment of his competition. "That there was some rude and illiterate people among them is no more than may be said of almost any society, and that some were vicious and depraved is equally true, but what there was of evil you saw on the surface for there was no effort at concealment," he said.

In 1831, Father Michael Muldoon became the priest of the town's Catholic church. Worship occurred indoors in a formal church in the plaza.

A replica depicting the way a San Felipe de Austin homestead may have looked before the town was burned. *Courtesy of the San Felipe de Austin State Historic Site via Facebook.*

Protestant worship, however, was conducted outside with a hodgepodge of ministers who preached to the congregations.

In general, religion had never become a serious focus for the settlers. In 1931, W.B. Dewees lamented the lack of sermons he'd heard in Texas.

> *The people of this country seem to have forgotten that there was such a commandment as "Remember the Sabbath Day." They spend this day visiting, driving stock and breaking mustangs.*

Education was, however, a founding principle of San Felipe de Austin. Austin had even wanted to build a college. He had $1,300 for its construction and a charter for its governance. A street had been named Collegio to denote its location, but the institution was never constructed.

Beyond Constitution Plaza was Military Plaza, where soldiers lived and artillery was stored. The Camp Santo Cemetery, the formal town burial site, was also in the plaza. Farther east, the medical center was called Hospital Plaza, or Hospicio Plaza.

San Felipe Speaks for Texas

Plantations began springing up almost immediately in the bottomlands. When they expanded, San Felipe de Austin turned into active trading center.

The town also had strong communication outlets.

Texas newspapers had a level of clout throughout the United States. First came the *Cotton Plant*, which became the *Texas Gazette* newspaper.

Later, Joseph Baker, Gail Borden Jr. and John P. Borden operated the *Telegraph and Texas Register*. Both newspapers were regularly relied on for posts and articles about Texas.

The three men announced the creation of their newspaper in the May 2, 1835 edition.

> *The* Telegraph *will be a tool to no party; but will fearlessly expose crime and political error wherever met with—its columns will be open to all; but the editors reserve to themselves the right of rejecting such communication as they deem unworthy or improper to be inserted. The* Telegraph *will ever be ready to advocate such principles and measures as have a tendency to promote union between Texans and the Mexican Confederation, as well as to oppose every shing tendiug* [sic] *to dissolve or weaken the connexion* [sic] *between them.*

John P. Borden. *Author's collection; from the public domain.*

Austin also had a great deal to do with the clout of San Felipe de Austin. He was not only the empresario of the town, but he was also the town's top ambassador. His efforts to attract settlers, especially Europeans, became more aggressive when reliable transportation arrived.

In the earliest days, keelboats transported goods between the town. Coastal ports circumvented the ravenous and treacherous Brazos River. When waters were too dangerous, goods went overland by wagon.

By the 1830s, however, more powerful steamboats began making their way up the river.

"Europeans wishing to settle in Austin's colony can procure every necessary information by applying or writing to S.F. Austin, or to Samuel M. Williams, who has been taken in by Austin as a partner in the last contract with government," wrote

Austin, who referred to himself in third person in his marketing materials, in December 1831. "Letters to those persons must be directed to the Town of San Felipe de Austin, Texas, and could be sent through some commercial house in New Orleans."

Williams was soon in charge of seven postal routes. The San Felipe de Austin Post Office became a centerpiece of Austin's colony.

Curiously, Williams would sometimes deal with postal mail from Americans who addressed their letters to the settlers of Saint Phillip, Town of Austin or, simply, Austin, Texas.

By 1835, only San Antonio was larger than San Felipe de Austin. The town was on the brink of westward expansion, Smithwick recalled.

"The old town formed the nucleus of the movement that eventuated in the extension of the great American Union in an unbroken plan from the Atlantic to the Pacific," he said.

In 1832 and 1833, the idea of governance in San Felipe de Austin was taking hold. Without a formal capital, leaders turned to Angelina's business, the Peyton Hotel. It became their unofficial chambers.

At some point, they considered building a brick capitol building in which to conduct their meetings. But like the college, it was never constructed.

After a false start, Texas self-governance occurred in a series of organized conventions. Leaders called them "consultations" so the Mexican government would not notice them.

At the November 3, 1835 consultation, the leaders could not gain a consensus about whether to go to war with Mexico. To work out their differences they divided themselves into two groups. One group would make the case to go to war. The other would draft the plan for a provisional government.

San Felipe de Austin was not only the capital of life in early Texas; it was a defining place where revolution percolated, friendships grew and enemies found each other.

4

THE INIMICAL CURSE

In 1831, Smithwick mounted his horse to begin his exile from San Felipe de Austin. Smithwick had helped a friend charged with murder escape from prison. For that decision, he was banished.

As he prepared to ride away, the settlers arrived with a bottle of whiskey and some glasses. They wanted him to toast the town for the last time.

He cursed it instead.

> *If there is an honest man in the place may he be conducted to a place of safety, and then may fire and brimstone be rained upon the iniquitous town.*

Five years later, in the spring of 1836, this happened.

In March 1836, as the Mexican preludes to war made the residents anxious, Houston was in San Felipe for the delegations. During the delegations, Houston was promoted from major general of the Texian army to its commander in chief.

With that promotion, he left the town to build his army in Gonzalez. On the way, Def Smith, Houston's spy, found Susannah Dickinson walking about twenty miles from town. She brought news of the fall of the Alamo. With her were her daughter, Angelina; Joe, the man enslaved by Travis; and Ben, a cook for the Mexican general Juan Almonte.

Then came the news of Goliad. Nicholas Descomps Labadie, the army doctor, recalled how the news affected the troops.

"The painful news of Fannin's defeat was brought into camp by one Peter Carr, whom Houston treated as a spy, putting him under guard," Labadie wrote in his diary. "We all, however, believed his report to be true, and it was corroborated by others the next day, after which the numbers in our camp began to diminish rapidly."

Panic began to spread. Every town was deserted as Texians transformed from settlers to refugees. They rushed toward the San Jacinto River in hopes of catching boats to Galveston and elsewhere.

Houston created a provisional army to guide them, but the Runaway Scrape was as brutal and demoralizing as the horror stories they'd heard. The trails were full of mud. The settlers were ill-prepared for the journey. Many died and were buried where they fell.

Meanwhile, Americans continued to pour into Gonzalez to join the Texian army, which soon grew to have 1,600 troops. They were full of ego and empty of discipline. Houston decided to return with them to San Felipe. He claimed he would meet the Mexicans there.

LAMAR'S ARRIVAL

Upon his return to San Felipe, Houston decided to position the troops at Groce's plantation outside the town. It was a move that caused some in his command to begin to openly criticize his "constant retreats."

Groce's plantation contained a ferry landing, and Houston soon learned that the *Yellowstone* steamer docked there. *Yellowstone* transported goods from Galveston and New Orleans. Its arrival meant the troops would probably have provisions. The steamer also meant the troops could reach the plantation via the river. That made for a faster and more efficient solution for everyone.

Lamar arrived at the plantation on the same *Yellowstone* cruise as the famed Twin Sister cannons, a gift from independence sympathizers in Cincinnati, Ohio. J.H. Kuykendall recalled the moment Lamar arrived.

> On the 12th, the army was ferried over the river (then very high) in the steamboat Yellowstone, and encamped a few hundred yards east of Groce's residence. Here we at length received what, since the beginning of the campaign had been a desideratum; namely, two beautiful, new, iron field pieces—the far famed "Twin Sisters." Here we were also joined by Mirabeau B. Lamar and a few other volunteers from the United States.

Groce's plantation. *Author's collection; from the public domain.*

The arrival of the cannons was the catalyst that changed the attitude of Captain Mosely Baker.

Baker made it clear he thought Houston's constant retreats were the reason the Runway Scrape was happening. He believed that if Houston had let the troops stand and fight, the settlers would have been safer.

Many others, including Lamar, thought this as well. Labadie remembered when Sidney Sherman found large amounts of unruly troop members.

> *As Houston had decided on marching up the river some twenty miles opposite Col. Groce's plantation, on giving orders to that effect, Sherman found two companies refused to come into line, and he sent a message to that effect to Houston, who had gone in advance with his staff.*

Houston sent word that they needed to obey, and if the commanders weren't going to do so, it's better to find it out now than later.

When Baker, who was in the First Regiment, refused to go to Groce's plantation, Houston told him to guard San Felipe instead. Houston also told the local townsmen to tend to their families while the troops continued to the plantation.

As Baker rallied his troops, Houston tapped six soldiers to guard the ferry and help Baker. One of them, Corporal Isaac L. Hill, took control of the ferry boat on March 26. Soon after, Baker arrived with his regiment, and everyone moved to the west bank. Houston left with the army.

Baker's troops dug a 124-yard-long trench underneath some cottonwood trees. The trench was shaped like an L. The longer section of the trench fronted the river.

As the troops worked, the residents presented Baker with the 1836 "independent flag." Stephen F. Austin, Branch T. Archer and William H. Wharton created the flag to drum up support in the United States. The *Texas Telegraph and Texas Register* described it:

> [The] *English Jack showing the origins of Anglo-Americans, thirteen stripes representing that most of the colonists are from the United States; the Star is Texas, the only state in Mexico retaining the least spark of the light of Liberty; tricolor is Mexican, showing that we once belonged to the confederacy; the whole flag is historic.*

The flag flew while the regiment was in San Felipe.

The troops stopped working on the trench around March 29. This was when Def Smith arrived with his report. He told Baker that Santa Anna's army was advancing toward San Felipe past the Colorado River.

Def Smith was a trusted spy for Houston. His ability to scout and handle sensitive missions became legend in early Texas.

Def Smith took John York with him to perform an earlier reconnaissance on Santa Anna and his army days.

Within a little time, they found Santa Anna's location. He was only twelve miles away at the San Bernard River.

On the strength of that report, Baker gathered the troops. He told them about a specific order he had received from Houston: "[He] had been instructed by Genl. [*sic*] Houston, upon the approach of the enemy, to burn

The San Felipe de Austin flag as seen flying over the San Jacinto monument in modern Texas. *Courtesy of the Texas Historical Commission.*

the town," Hill remembered. "[And] that in obedience to said order the company would proceed to reduce it to ashes."

Hill wrote the troops crossed the river and arrived in town at about 8:00 p.m. while Baker "harangued" them.

"He stated, in substance, that he thought it was bad policy to burn the town but that Genl. [*sic*] Houston was inimical to him and would avail himself of any plausable pretext to injure him," Hill wrote. "He was therefore determined to execute his orders to the letter."

All I Love Is There

First, Baker burned his own office, which Hill said lit up the night sky. The townspeople followed Baker's example.

"The houses were of wood and the conflagration was rapid and brilliant," he said.

Hill believed most merchants, except William P. Huff, had left and that only their clerks were still in town, but he was wrong. Many residents were still there.

The troops asked the clerks if they could take the goods as supplies, but the clerks refused. The clerks burned the stores instead, Hill remembered.

"A large amount of goods were destroyed by this conflagration," he wrote.

It took Baker, his troops and the townspeople hours to reduce San Felipe to ashes. They burned all the town's homes and businesses. Huff saw Gail Borden burn not just his own store but also the Butler Hotel. Huff recalled Borden saying that even though it was hard to do, he would follow the orders.

Hill said the men and troops stayed until they were sure the town would be nothing but ashes.

"It was nearly midnight and the town was almost consumed, when the company returned to camp," Hill wrote.

Before the flames erupted, Baker moved the settlers to his camp. Angelina Peyton was among them. She recalled later that she heard the destruction for hours.

"We camped four miles from the river and heard at intervals the popping of spirits, the powder in our burning homes," she recalled.

Peyton was with her two children, Alexander and Meg. Her husband died before the siege. By one account, Meg was a beautiful child and many of the town leaders adored her. Travis and Austin were among her fans.

After her husband's death, Angelina gathered a small staff and opened the Peyton Hotel. That hotel then became the headquarters for the revolution.

When Baker told her he had to get the settlers to the other side of the Brazos, she pleaded with him not to destroy her livelihood. She watched her neighbors walk on foot and wade through mud up to their knees as they followed his orders.

She had said she was the last woman to leave San Felipe.

"And I said to Capt. Baker as I cast a long and lingering look over my deserted home, 'Don't burn the town. All I love is there.'"

The Canoe That Did Not Return

The next morning, the troops began working on the entrancement again, and Baker wrote another letter to Houston. He read it to Hill and others before he sent it, because he was worried of how it would be received.

"General Houston is inimical to me," Baker started. "I have to be very cautious. I will read you this letter."

Hill remembered, "It stated, in substance, that having received intelligence that the enemy had crossed the Colorado and were advancing towards San Felipe, he had, in obedience to the order of the commander-in-chief, burned the town."

Houston replied to him the same day and told Baker he approved. Hill wrote that Baker read Houston's reply to them as well.

In a few days, more settlers joined Baker's troops and their number swelled to almost 125. They waited for Santa Anna by the hour.

Then Baker appointed picket guards. Hill remembered when he was chosen.

On the evening of the 5th Apl. [sic] James M. Bell, William Simpson and myself were selected by Captain Baker for what was deemed a perilous service, namely, to act as a picket guard the ensuing night on the San Felipe side of the river. We crossed the river—then very high—in a canoe which Captain Baker ordered should be sent back immediately—so fearful was he of its falling into the hands of the enemy and affording them the means of crossing the river and surprising his camp.

They did not follow orders. They kept the canoe and locked it to a tree. Then they "proceeded on and posted ourselves on a gentle eminence in the prairie a little west of the site of the main part of the town and about three-fourths of a mile from the ferry."

Hill and Bell went to sleep with the expectation that Simpson would wake them up in the morning. Instead, Simpson began foraging in a nearby garden for vegetables. The Mexican cavalry surprised him.

They seemed determined to capture him and soon did, according to Hill. The two sleeping men were awakened by the chase. They started a mad dash to the ferry, although Bell tried to convince Hill to stand and fight.

"The Mexicans discovered us before we had got half way [sic] and instantly the whole squadron spurred their horses in pursuit of us," Hill wrote. "We followed the high road which passed a little to the right of the head of a ravine."

They were saved when the cavalry became too ambitious. Instead of following them, the troops headed too far to the left of the ravine to try to cut them off. Their horses couldn't make it through, and the cavalry had to detour.

"Yet, we would still have been lost had I listened to the rash proposition of my companion to face the enemy and fight!" Hill wrote.

"We had scarcely got into the canoe and pushed it from the shore when the Mexicans were on the bank and shooting at us," he recalled. "They fired two or three rounds before we reached the opposite shore and one of them bade us in good English, 'Bring back that boat!'"

Watching from the other riverbank, Baker thought he was watching a Texian spy company. Then he saw the Mexicans firing at the men. Baker's troops returned fire, and the cavalry left.

Thirty minutes later, Hill said the Mexican army returned. They made camp on the southwest side of the burned town, about five hundred yards from the ferry.

In response, Baker moved the troops one-fourth of a mile up the river. He left some troops, including Hill, in the entrenchment. Texian sentinels lined the river for one mile above and below the ditch.

On April 7, Hill woke up in the entrenchment to the sound of a booming cannon. It was near the Commercial Square, or what used to be that section of town.

"Many rounds of roundshot, grape and cannister were discharged at us, throwing the sand upon us and knocking the bark from the cottonwood trees that extended their branches over us," he wrote.

Meanwhile, Baker sank the ferry under Houston's orders.

The battle continued until April 10, when the Mexican army left.

It was on that day that Captain John Byrd and a company of mounted troops rode up to Baker. Byrd said Houston told him to take over the command of San Felipe. Baker and his regimen had orders to return to Groce's plantation.

Baker didn't immediately do this.

Instead, he put it to the vote of the troops, Hill said.

He said he had defended the crossing until the Mexican army had departed and he could not see the necessity of remaining any longer in that position— but submitted it to the men whether they would remain or march to rejoin the army.

With a rising vote from the troops, Baker gave the order and the men marched on.

As Baker and his troops marched to rejoin Houston, they camped at Iron's Creek. Runaway Scrape refugees from Fort Bend walked within a mile of them. Baker went to see them.

When the captain returned, he was overwhelmed with emotion.

"He was much affected by the distress he had witnessed," Hill wrote. "[A] mong the women and children, a number of whom were travelling [*sic*] on foot. Learning from one of the ladies that she had been insulted by a negro man, he sought the negro and intended, had he found him, to run him through his sword. Captain Baker wept."

THE CURSE FULFILLED

Around that same time, Def Smith realized that he had not seen Santa Anna at the San Bernard River.

When the Mexican army didn't show up until three days after the town burned, he and York began to question themselves.

They soon realized they had seen cattle watering at the river and not an imposing army.

The men realized that they had worn out their horses from the constant scouting they had been doing. The animals were almost broken down and needed rest. As a result, the men didn't go close to the river.

They also didn't have their field glasses to help them view what they were looking at.

Both men were upset when they realized they had mistaken the wild cattle for the Mexican army.

It was the only time Def Smith ever returned to camp with a bad report.

Houston denied for a long time that he had given any order to burn the town, even though he'd given similar orders before.

On the retreat from Gonzalez, he ordered the troops to burn the town so Santa Anna would not be able to rummage it and gather supplies.

In the case of San Felipe, Houston said for years, he had acted otherwise.

Labadie went to visit Houston after the burning of San Felipe with their mutual friend J.N. Moreland. While they were there, Houston brought up the burning of San Felipe.

"Turning towards us he said: 'Moreland, did you ever hear me give orders to burn the town of San Felipe?' His reply was: 'General, I have no recollection of it.' 'Yet they blame me for it,' said Houston," recalled Labadie.

Many years later, in 1844, Baker and Houston engaged in another battle—albeit a political one. Baker wrote a scathing letter to Houston about his leadership and actions at San Felipe.

He characterized the retreat to Groce's plantation as a retreat "to a lake."

"Your army followed you with the exception of my company," Baker wrote years later. "Satisfied that you had no intention to fight, I indignantly refused longer to follow you....You put your army in motion and when you found that I would no longer be led by you, you rode back to me in person and gave me orders to take post opposite San Felipe with my command, and gave me orders to burn the town on the approach of the enemy," he emphatically wrote.

Hill also addressed the controversy head-on.

Neither Captain Baker's men nor the people of the town doubted that it was destroyed by order of the commander-in-chief.

Angelina agreed with Hill and Baker. She would never forget the burning of the town she had loved and the man who said he didn't order its destruction.

5

SHERMAN'S SKIRMISH
AT SAN JACINTO

Between Groce's plantation and San Jacinto, the troops split into two separate camps. Those who supported Houston's battlefield decisions were pitted against those who did not.

Private James Tarleton, who served under Baker, wrote a letter to his brother in Kentucky about how Houston's constant retreats had worn on the troops who were itching to fight.

"Our army under the command of Gen. Sam Houston became tired of retreating, and expressed a great anxiety to be led to meet the enemy at once to decide the fate of Texas," he wrote.

Lamar had fallen into the Lieutenant Colonel Sidney Sherman camp, which questioned virtually every decision Houston made and even invited outright mutiny under the commander's nose.

Many times, Houston let the mutiny rhetoric flourish rather than quash it, even though he had the authority to do so.

The battle preparations occurred against the natural beauty that engulfed San Jacinto. Behind the camp was Buffalo Bayou, with groves of giant live oaks with spreading limbs. Soft gray moss festooned their vivid green leaves.

For two miles rolled a fertile prairie dotted with tall grasses and small gathering of trees. The gulf marshes of the bay were thick and full of swampy timber, according to early Texas historian Dudley Wooten.

The wet, and late spring was now ripening into early summer, the atmosphere was soft and balmy, the trees and grass were fresh and fragrant,

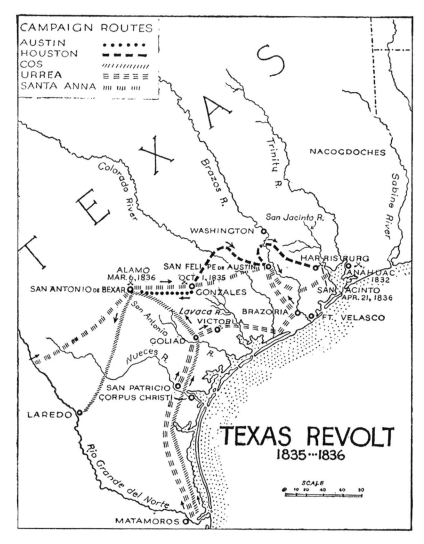

A map that shows the campaign routes in the Siege of 1836. *Author's collection; from the public domain.*

and the whole scene was full of those sights and sounds that make life sweet and hope strong in human breasts.

It was in this garden of luxurious plants and fauna that Houston questioned himself. He was perplexed about how to move forward with ragtag troops who were untrained in battlefield fundamentals.

Left: Sidney Sherman. *Courtesy of the Texas State Library and Archives Commission.*

Right: Thomas Rusk. *Courtesy of the Texas State Library and Archives Commission.*

Years later, he revealed that he pondered whether he should have simply stayed at Gonzalez and trained the troops. He wondered if his retreat campaign was the right decision.

For example, on the day Houston arrived at Gonzalez, he mulled that he had found 374 men "without two days' provisions, many without arms, and others without any ammunition."

In Gonzalez, he decided to organize the troops into regiments. He divided the troops between Lieutenant Colonel Sidney Sherman, Colonel Edward Burleson and Major Alexander Somervell. He questioned in the following years if he should have trained each man in "the first principle of the drill" before he let them command.

In other words, Houston said he later realized that he expected untrained leaders to command huge amounts of troops who had never learned the discipline of battle.

Nonetheless, at Groce's plantation, Houston promoted Sherman to colonel of the Second Regiment. Whispers spread that Houston never intended to fight Santa Anna.

The rebel government had the same thoughts about Houston as his mutiny-leaning troops. Government leaders had serious concerns that Houston was a true coward.

David Burnet, the president of the rebel provisional government during the war, told Houston to fight. "Sir: The enemy are laughing you to scorn. You must fight them. You must retreat no further. The country expects you to fight. The salvation of the country depends on your doing so," Burnet said.

Houston dug in his heels and gave a fiery reply.

> *I have kept the army together under most discouraging circumstances, and I hope a just and wise God, in whom I have always believed, will yet save Texas. I am sorry that I am so wicked, for the "prayers of the righteous shall prevail." That you are so, I have no doubt, and hope that Heaven as such, will…crown your efforts with success on behalf of Texas and humanity.*

Burnet decided to send Secretary of War Thomas Rusk to see if he could instill some courage in the commander.

WET INK

Houston's decision to fight didn't come immediately. He didn't make the decision until Santa Anna's own words hit him in the face.

The predicament presented itself when Def Smith and a captain came back with a pair of couriers. One carried a pile of letters to Santa Anna hailing him as the emperor of Mexico.

The other carried something more important. It was a letter from Santa Anna to Houston. As someone read it to Houston, the ink was still wet.

Houston and Rusk retreated to discuss the letter and the wet ink. If Santa Anna was so close that the ink had not even dried on a letter to him, he was as close as he'd ever get.

The two men said little while Houston concluded the obvious.

"We need not talk," he said to Rusk. "[Y]ou think we ought to fight and I think so too."

Shortly after their meeting, Houston heard that a popular regiment leader told his troops, "Boys, Houston don't intend to fight; follow me and you shall have enough of it."

In answer to the report of open mutiny, Houston said, "I'll cure this mischief directly."

HEROIC LAMAR

Meanwhile, Sherman was so excited to fight, he didn't want to wait for Houston to tell him what to do. The night before the famed battle, he asked Houston to let him sneak into the Mexican camp and steal the "brass twelve-pounder" cannon. The cannon had been hurling grapeshot and canister at them. They hurled their responses from the Twin Sisters cannons.

A back-and-forth began between Sherman and Houston, with Houston eventually relenting.

Some pro-Houston supporters later said they believed Sherman didn't think Houston would ever fight Santa Anna. Others would claim that Sherman wanted to create a ruse that would force Houston to engage.

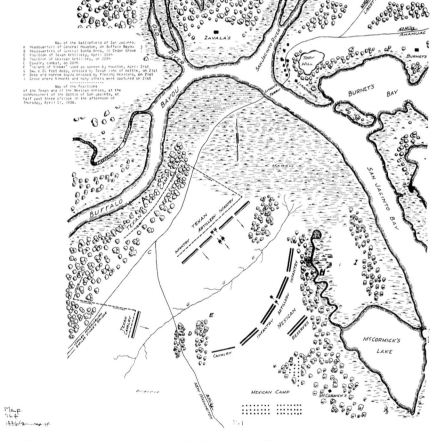

San Jacinto battle camp map. *Author's collection; from the public domain.*

Houston's agreement with Sherman had some conditions. Sherman could not go within range of the Mexican troops. Houston didn't want a fight to start. The cavalry and artillery were supposed to stay behind a grove of trees.

Lamar and Rusk were among those who joined Sherman's skirmish.

"The reconnoitering party had hardly disappeared, before the sound of firing in that direction was heard," Crane wrote. "In a single moment a suspicion of Sherman's real design flashed over Houston's mind; he mounted his horse and rode straight to the scene of action."

Once Sherman began his skirmish, a disciplined Mexican army outwitted him. They operated with precise military tactics, according to Crane. Sherman's troops launched a disorganized attack that ended in the death of Olwyns J. Trask.

The Mexicans also killed several Texian horses; this included the mounts for Rusk and Walter Lane, a nineteen-year-old teen.

When the two were being bombarded with Mexican cannon fire, Lamar rushed to save both men. This rescue was so heroic that the Mexicans stopped for a moment to salute him.

By the time Houston reached Sherman's retreat, the commander found the wounded troops. They delivered Trask's dead body to him on horseback.

"Houston was incensed, for all this had been done in direct violation of his orders, and two of his Spartan soldiers borne bleeding by, were the only fruits that had followed," Crane wrote.

He was incredulous that years later, Sherman would charge that Houston had set him up to be cut off. Troop member Robert Coleman, who was Houston's aide-de-camp, would levy even more serious charges in the years to come.

He would charge that Houston was so jealous of Sherman that he wanted him to die.

THE PIVOT POINT

Houston and Lamar reached an important moment in their relationship after Sherman's skirmish.

While many would eventually question Lamar's pragmatism as a leader, few would ever doubt Lamar's bravery or battlefield skills after Sherman's skirmish.

The troops at San Jacinto celebrated him in the moments afterward. The day after the skirmish, Houston named Lamar the commander of the sixty-one-member cavalry.

Houston wrote to David Burnet that Lamar's "gallant and daring conduct" during the skirmish at San Jacinto was the reason for his promotion. Lamar did not disappoint during the battle the next day.

Our cavalry, sixty-one in number, commanded by Colonel Mirabeau B. Lamar, whose gallant and daring conduct on the previous day had attracted the admiration of his comrades and called him to that station, placed on our right, completed our line. Our cavalry was first dispatched to the front of the enemy's left, for the purpose of attracting their notice, whilst an extensive island of timber afforded us an opportunity of concentrating our forces and deploying from that point, agreeably to the previous design of the troops. Every evolution was performed with alacrity, the whole advancing rapidly in line and through an open prairie, without any protection whatever for our men.

With the skirmish finished, thoughts turned to the impending battle. One young man named Benjamin Rice Brigham was especially excited.

Brigham wanted to give up his guard duty so he could sleep well before the battle.

"Boys," he said, "I've stood guard two nights, and am detailed for the third. I want to be in the battle tomorrow. Will somebody take my place tonight?"

F.J. Cooke offered to do so, and Brigham went to sleep.

The next morning, Houston held a council of war, where he walked among the troops as they gathered around campfires.

He asked if they wanted to fight.

"We replied with a shout that we were most anxious to do so," James Washington Winters, a member of Sherman's division under Captain William Ware, wrote.

"Then Houston replied, 'Very well, get your dinners and I will lead you into the fight, and if you whip them every one of you shall be a captain,'" Winters continued.

Winters recalled that Houston was reluctant to believe the troops were ready to fight. He knew the men had split into factions over his leadership.

Above: In modern Texas, NASA jets fly over the San Jacinto monument, providing an overview of the battlefield. *Courtesy of NASA.*

Left: John Winters. *Author's collection; from the public domain.*

Houston preferred the opinions of the men themselves, feeling that before hazarding battle he must find whether they would enter the engagement with a will. For the men had marched so long with out [sic] *food or rest that, perhaps, they might not be physically prepared.*

After dinner, the men were ready for battle.

We Obeyed the Impulse of Our Feelings

"On beginning the battle, before we got in sight of the Mexicans, they began firing at us," Winters remembered.

Once Winters's regiment reached the Mexicans, they found spent cartridges. They later determined that each Mexican troop had fired at least five times at each one of the Texians.

Winters then saw that Lamar's cavalry were in hot pursuit of the Mexican cavalry, which broke into disarray as they ran from Lamar's troops.

Then he noticed Houston rushing past the Mexican camp. The commander began riding his third horse in the battle. Two others had been killed under him. Winter did not know that by that time, Houston had also been shot. A musket ball had hit a bone right above his ankle.

"I never heard any halt ordered," Winter said. "We never halted. The battle was won in fifteen or eighteen minutes."

Tarleton also recalled that he had seen Houston continue to fight after he was wounded.

"I had almost forgotten to state that in our glorious and triumphant battle, Gen. Houston was wounded in his left ancle [*sic*] and I seize this occasion to state that on the field he appeared, collected and fearlessly brave," Tarleton wrote.

Winters said after the fight ended, Houston ordered the men to form a line and march to camp. The unruly troops ignored him.

[B]ut we payed [sic] *no attention to him, as we were all shaking hands and rejoicing over the victory. Houston gave the order three times and still the men payed* [sic] *no attention to him. And he turned his horse around and said "Men, I can gain victories with you, but damn your manners" and rode on to camp.*

The Battlefield of San Jacinto. *Courtesy of Henry Arthur McArdle.*

Tarleton was more direct in his account and charged that Houston never gave any order. He had made a request.

> *I had but one fault to find with him, and that was that he requested us to cease pursuit and return to camp whilse [sic] the enemy was in sight and flying before us. I have no doubt he thought he was right in so doing, but fortunately for the county, he might as well attempt to still the billows of the raging deep. If we had obeyed his request—for it was not an order— Santa Anna and his right hand man, Almonti and Cos, with 400 of the prisoners, might have escaped, and hundreds who were afterwards slain, would perhaps have enabled the despot to continue his crusade for months to come, and to harass if not to subjugate the country.*

In closing, Tarleton admitted the troops didn't respect Houston's authority, and he was glad of it.

> *We obeyed no order and no command but the impulse of our own feelings. We came, we saw, we conquered; and I thank God that I was one of the few who did achieve this great and glorious victory.*

BRIGHAM DIES

When Lamar arrived back at camp, he saw Brigham in the throes of death. He'd fallen early in the battle and within a few hours, he died. Lamar was moved deeply and retired to his tent, where he wrote a poem to process his feelings.

San Jacinto
by Mirabeau Lamar

Beautiful in death
The soldier's corpse appears,
Embalmed by fond affection's breath
And bathed in his country's tears.

Lo, the battle forms
Its terrible array,
Like clashing clouds in mountain storms
That thunder on their way.

The rushing armies meet,
And while they pour their breath,
The strong earth trembles at their feet,
And day grows dim with death.

Now launch upon the foe
The lightnings of your rage!
Strike the assailing tyrants low,
The monsters of the age!

They yield! They break! They fly!
The victory is won!
Pursue! They faint, they fall, they die!
O stay! The work is done.

Mourn the death of those
Who for their country die,
Sink on her bosom for repose,
And triumph where they lie.
Laurels for those who bled,

The living hero's due.
But holier wreaths will crown the dead
A grateful nation's love!

While Houston might have been impressed with Lamar at the Battle of San Jacinto, Houston did not impress Lamar at all.

Lamar remembered, years later, a conversation he had with Houston the day after his promotion.

"Sometime after the council of war, I met Gen. Houston, and expressed to him the strong desire of the army to make battle," Lamar remembered. "He replied merely as follows: 'Sir, can I whip Santa Anna and his whole army by myself? Would you have me attack them alone? The officers are all opposed to fighting, and so are the men. I have always been ready to fight but the army has not, and how can I battle?'"

The conversation restarted the day of the attack.

"At the moment we were all preparing for battle, and his lines were actually forming, Houston came to me and said, 'Col. Lamar, do you really think we ought to fight?'"

According to Winters, Houston had serious concerns for the welfare of the troops.

Lamar interpreted the conversation as the words of a true coward.

EL PRESIDENTE ARRIVES IN CAMP

A year after the Battle of San Jacinto, Santa Anna wrote in his report that he decided to escape capture at the battle when he realized that all his generals had been wounded or killed. He wrote that his troops abandoned their posts.

> [T]*he enemy taking advantage of the opportunity, carried their charge forward rapidly, and shouting madly, secured a victory in a few minutes which they did not dream was possible. All hope was lost, with everyone escaping as best he could, my despair was as a great as the danger I was in.*
>
> *A servant of my aide-de-camp, Juan Bringas, with noble kindness offered me the horse of his master, and earnestly pleaded that I save myself. I looked about for my escort and was told by two dragoons who were hurriedly saddling their horses that their companions and officers had fled.*

A print of a sketch by an unknown artist depicting Santa Anna's surrender to General Sam Houston during the Texas Revolution; it also lists those in attendance. *Courtesy of the Portal of Texas History.*

Santa Anna said he decided to head to Thompson's Crossing, where he remembered Filisola was staying. Houston's troops rushed after him and almost captured him near Vince's Bridge. They lost him when he got off his horse to hide in a small grove of pine trees until nightfall.

> *The coming of night permitted me to evade their vigilance. The hope of rejoining the army and of vindicating its honor gave me strength to cross the creek with water above my waist, and I continued on route afoot. In an abandoned house I found some clothes which I exchanged for wet ones.*

The day after the battle, the Texian troops prepared to scour the countryside to find Santa Anna.

Houston told them, "You will find the Hero of Tampico, if you find him at all, making his retreat on all fours, and he will be dressed as bad at least as a common soldier. Examine every man you find, closely."

Crane recalled that the capture happened just like Houston said it would.

> *About three o'clock in the afternoon, Lt. J.A. Sylvester, a volunteer from Cincinnati, Joel W. Robison, now of Fayette Co., John Thompson, and others were riding over the prairie. They espied [sic] a man making his*

Santa Anna. *Courtesy of the Texas State Library and Archives Commission.*

way toward Vince's bridge. They pursued him, whereupon he fell down in the grass.

Sylvester rushed toward the man and also fell. His horse almost trampled him as he realized the man he had found was Santa Anna.

According to Crane, the Mexican leader was "disguised in a miserable rustic dress, wearing a skin cap, a round jacket, pantaloons of blue domestic cotton, and a pair of coarse soldier's shoes, he sprang to his feet, and without the slightest apparent surprise looked his captor full in the face."

The troops noticed that underneath his disguise, Santa Anna wore a fine linen shirt, which gave his status away.

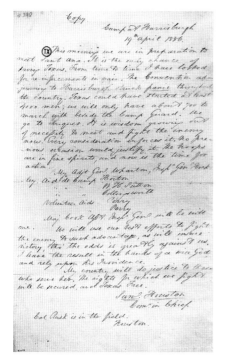

Sam Houston's letter about meeting Santa Anna on the battlefield. *Courtesy of the Texas State Library and Archives Commission.*

Sylvester was polite and tipped his hat as he said, "You are an officer, I perceive, sir?"

Crane claimed that Santa Anna replied with, "No, soldier."

Later, Santa Anna admitted he had lied to him.

> *Not recognizing me because of my clothes, they asked me if I had seen General Santa Anna. I replied that he was ahead of me and this happy thought saved me from being assassinated on the spot as I was found out later.*

As Santa Anna entered camp and rode past the Mexican prisoners, they lifted their caps. Cries of "El Presidente!" rose into the air, and his ruse ended.

Houston, who was not sleeping well after his battle injury, was resting in a light sleep on the ground. When the troops marched Santa Anna into the camp, Santa Anna came in behind them.

Houston woke up and turned over to come face to face with Santa Anna. Crane wrote that the royal placed his right hand on his heart, extended his left arm and said, "I am General Antonio Lopez de Santa

Anna, President of the Mexican Republic, and I claim to be your prisoner of war."

Houston offered him the only seat in the camp, a box, and replied, "Ah! General Santa Anna, take a seat; I am glad to see you."

6

MUTINY AT VICTORIA

For Santa Anna's first meeting with Houston, he dressed like he was going to a gala. He wore an elegant outfit while Houston wore a plain "old black coat, snuff-colored pantaloons, a black-velvet vest, a fur cap, a worn-out pair of boots" and a curved sword that hung from buckskin thongs, Crane wrote.

The Mexican general acted like he was a gracious guest at a gala that Houston was hosting. Santa Anna inquired about Houston's health and his battle wound. Houston, like a good host, politely conversed about the topic.

Then Santa Anna asked to negotiate his release.

From that moment on, Houston had a witness at every meeting he had with the man. Most of the time, the witness was Rusk.

At one point, Santa Anna wrote his proposal, which Houston declined to discuss, in pencil. Houston said Texas was now ruled by the rebel government and that they had been summoned to negotiate with him.

Santa Anna was not interested in that at all.

"Santa Anna manifested perfect willingness to act with military men, and exhibited great aversion against any negotiations with civilians," Crane wrote.

Houston and Rusk discussed only the retreat of the remaining Mexican troops. Santa Anna agreed to call one.

Upon their arrival, President Burnet and the rebel government agreed to formalize this. Santa Anna ordered the retreat through Texas.

Crane recounted that Houston's wound had gotten worse. Soon after the agreement, Houston decided to allow the troops to vote for a brigadier general.

They chose Rusk. Houston appointed him on May 5, 1836.

Lamar was appointed secretary of war to fill the vacancy in the cabinet. One of his first acts—with Burnet's blessing—was to try to stop Houston's efforts to sail to Galveston. Then Houston wanted to sail onto New Orleans for medical treatment, according to Crane.

> As there was no medicine in the camp, no comforts for a wounded man, it was necessary to visit New Orleans to secure such medical aid as would save his life. Houston applied to the Cabinet for a passage. The application was sternly refused, and it seemed that the Commander-in-Chief was about to be left to die—in sight of the field of San Jacinto.

The steamboat captain who brought Burnet and the rebel leaders saw what happened. He took Houston's hands and said the boat would not leave shore without him. A few of Houston's staff followed, but when his surgeon general Dr. Ewing followed, Lamar stopped him. Lamar told him that if he followed Houston, he would be discharged from service.

Crane wrote that Houston told the man, "I am sorry, my dear fellow, for I have nothing to promise you in the future, and you know I am poor; so you had better not incur the displeasure of the new Secretary of War."

Like the troops at the battle, Ewing ignored Houston's authority and followed him aboard. Lamar discharged him from service, with Burnet's blessing.

Meanwhile, Santa Anna, who was also on board as a captive, heard about the trouble getting Houston on board and became distraught. Crane recounted that whenever Santa Anna saw Houston, he always became immediately happy. The Mexican general enjoyed his visits with Houston.

The anti-Houston faction described Houston's manners with Santa Anna in much the same way. They said Houston acted like a puppy-eyed schoolgirl around Santa Anna.

Back on land, Lamar quickly moved to have Santa Anna executed. On May 12, he wrote to President Burnet and the cabinet. He implored them to stop thinking of Santa Anna as a prisoner of war.

A loud and sizable group had called for Santa Anna to be executed from the moment he was captured on the battlefield. Houston had some of these unruly voices exiled from the battlegrounds. Lamar was not among them, and now Lamar had the ability to make their opinions heard.

Lamar made the case that Santa Anna was a murderer. He made references to the deaths of Fannin and the Georgia Battalion without mentioning their names.

A chieftain battling for what he conceives to be the rights of his country, however mistaken in his views, may be privileged to make hot and vigorous war upon the foe; but, when in violation of all principles of civilized conflict, he avows and acts upon the revolting policey [sic] of extermination and rapine, slaying the surrendering and plundering whom he slays, he forfeits the commisseration [sic] of mankind by sinking the character of the hero into that of an abhorred murderer.

Some would assent to the justice of the sentence of death, but were willing to waive its execution for certain advantages which might flow to the country from a wise and judicious action. He asked what surety had they that any stipulations would be carried out.

What he assents to while a prisoner, he may reject when a free-man [sic]. Indeed, the idea of treating with a man in our power, who views freedom in acquiescence, and death in opposition, seems to me more worthy of ridicule than refutation.

Two days later, an agreement with Santa Anna was reached. The Mexican general would be released from Vera Cruz.

That's when those who wanted Santa Anna executed began to rattle their cages. In particular, the agreement did not appease a contingent from Louisiana.

On June 3, Thomas Jefferson Green arrived with 230 volunteers from New Orleans. They had plans to stop the release and force an execution.

Lamar did not support Green, even though they both wanted Santa Anna to die. Lamar believed that if the general could not be executed, Santa Anna should agree to the exchange of prisoners and other provisions. The agreement included some of Lamar's suggestions, so he supported it.

The matter of whether to execute Santa Anna divided Texas. So much was riding on whether the general lived or died that the United States even interjected on the matter. Houston was the country's ambassador.

U.S. President Andrew Jackson wrote on September 4, 1836, that Santa Anna was still popular with the Mexican people. Furthermore, Texas had nothing to fear. The military would not do anything if "their favorite general" was alive and in custody.

"Let not his blood be shed unless imperious necessity demands it, as a retaliation for future Mexican massacres," Jackson wrote Houston.

Generals in the American army agreed. They told Houston that any thought of a trial and execution would tarnish the good legacy of the rebels.

U.S. general Edmund P. Gaines wrote on August 3, 1836, that the legacy of the Texas Revolution would be determined by the way Santa Anna was treated.

> *No inconsiderable portion of your fame, resulting from your late campaign, the great victory of San Jacinto, will be found in the magnanimity and moral courage displayed by you in preserving the lives of your prisoners, and more especially the life of President Santa Anna, when taken in connection with the great provocation given in his previous conduct at the Alamo and at Goliad. The government and the infant republic of Texas will derive imperishable fame from their and your forbearance in this case.*

Houston heard about these plans while he was in New Orleans and responded quickly. He wrote a letter that an execution would put Americans who live in Mexico at great harm.

Houston argued that an execution would make the Texas–United States relationship unstable. It could cause the deaths of the Texas prisoners who were still in Mexico's custody. Problems could arise for the American clergy who were there as well.

Besides, it was just un-Texan. In fact, he wrote that he couldn't believe the statement when he heard it, because "it is obviously contrary to the true policy of Texas."

Executing Santa Anna might feel good in the moment, but it would destroy any chances of a strong republic.

"Texas, to be respected, must be considerate, politic, and just in her actions. Santa Anna, living and secured beyond all danger of escape, in the eastern section of Texas (as I first suggested), may be of incalculable advantage to Texas in her present crisis," Houston said. "I, therefore, Commander-in-Chief of the army of the Republic, do solemnly protest against the trial, sentence, and execution of General Antonio Lopez de Santa Anna, President of the Republic of Mexico, until the relations in which we are to stand to the United States shall be ascertained."

As Houston and Lamar made their cases about Santa Anna, Rusk led the Mexican retreat.

He sent 250 troops to deliver the message to Mexican general Filisola. "With a confused, upset and demoralized army," Crane wrote, Filisola executed the order under the white flag of truce.

Under Rusk's leadership, the army also traveled to Goliad and buried the bones of Fannin and the Georgia Battalion; then they established a military headquarters in Victoria.

THOUSANDS OF UNRULY TROOPS

The Mexican retreat was hurried and arduous. It took most of summer as well as some of the autumn of 1836, Crane wrote.

"Horses, mules, baggage-wagons, and sick soldiers were scattered along the path of the flying division, indicating the great panic under which the retreat had been made. To reach the Colorado the march was through a low, flat, wet prairie," said Crane.

It was also an uncertain retreat. From the moment Texas had Santa Anna, the leaders were worried about a second Mexican invasion. They felt rushed to defend the fledgling republic and its new government.

Felix Huston capitalized on those concerns. The jolly and calculating Mississippian showed up in Victoria with up to seven hundred troops. They all hoped to join the second war effort.

From the moment the troops arrived, Huston began vying for their command. He had a competition from Green.

By July, the number of troops in Victoria swelled to 2,300. They were unruly, and a full-scale mutiny was percolating to a boil.

Houston rallied some of these troops himself from his hospital bed in New Orleans.

In New Orleans, Crane wrote, the general arrived frail. He appeared almost dead. Throngs of supporters met the "near corpse." A band even played.

In a few weeks, however, Houston got stronger and, against medical advice, began making plans to return to Texas. He also grew concerned about a second Mexican invasion.

At New Orleans, Natchitoches [sic], and San Augustine, demonstrations of great respect had been made, and dinners offered to him, all of which compliments he declined; but when the report of the advance of the enemy had brought together a vast concourse of people at San Augustine, he was taken to the meeting resting on his crutches, and delivered so effective and arousing an address, that in two days one hundred and sixty men took up their march for the frontier.

HOUSTON IN ABSENTIA

The swell of army volunteers at Victoria created a frenzy of its own. They needed a clear leader.

"The army undoubtedly fell into a state of mutiny," Asa Kryus Christian wrote in 1922 during his doctorate studies at the University of Austin. "Each of the leaders of volunteers was intriguing for the chief command. Some of the soldiers held that Sam Houston was still in command though absent, and refused to obey the orders of Rusk. It was under these circumstances that Rusk appealed to the President and Cabinet to appoint a commander-in-chief of the army."

Rusk's choice was Huston. Huston was popular with the troops. He had been an advocate and fundraiser for Texas Independence. He also had a strong penchant as a military opportunist and an aggressive rebel.

However, President Burnet wanted the brave, competent and heroic Lamar. Within weeks of being appointed secretary of war, Lamar was heading to Victoria to assume the role Houston previously held. Lamar was going to become the major general and commander-in-chief of the army.

Burnet appointed him on June 25. The date was mere weeks after Lamar told Green he did not support his efforts to execute Santa Anna.

On the way, Lamar had stopped in Brazoria to make plans to handle the threat of another Mexican invasion. He also made provisions for army supplies. He read numerous letters of congratulations.

On July 14, Lamar arrived at the Guadalupe camp near Victoria. Huston promptly announced that Lamar had arrived with staunch opposition of his command.

Huston, who had been at camp since July 4, said he was acting on behalf of the troops, Crane wrote. Depending on what story was being told, Huston was either genuine in his assertion or had been duplicitous from the beginning.

> *Huston said, all present were willing to acknowledge the merits of Lamar, but that they denied the power of the Cabinet to supersede General Houston and they would not consent to the destruction of General Rusk. He suggested the appointment of a committee to meet General Lamar and acquaint him with the desires of the officers.*

This was done, and a resolution was drawn up to create the perimeters the troops would use to "learn about Lamar." The resolution stated:

Resolved, That this meeting highly appreciate the gallantry and worth of General Lamar, and will be at all times ready to receive him with the cordiality and respect due to his personal and military acquirements.

Resolved, That Colonel B.F. Smith and Colonel H. Millard be appointed a committee to wait on General Lamar, and tender him the respects of this meeting, and inform him that, there being some question of the propriety of his appointment by the President as major-general of the Texan army, by which he is directed to assume the chief command of the army, he is requested by the officers present not to act in his official capacity of major-general until the subject may be more maturely considered by the meeting of the officers of the army.

With this unexpected development, Lamar addressed the troops. He discussed his concern that Mexico would invade again. He mentioned his role in the Battle of San Jacinto. He claimed he was uninterested in leading an army that didn't want him. He would "cheerfully take his place in the ranks."

After a few other speeches, including ones from Green, Huston and Rusk, the troops voted.

Lamar gained 179 votes. The troops cast "probably 1,500 against him," Christian wrote.

Most of the opponents favored Sam Houston as their commander.

Although Lamar appeared conciliatory during the vote, he did not take the incident lightly. He realized that Rusk and Huston had worked together to undermine him. He wrote about his anger in a letter to President Burnet on July 17.

Everything is in the utmost confusion and rebellion. On my arrival I was informed that I could not be recognized as Commander in Chief. I proposed to speak to the soldiers, and did so, but was answered by Rusk, Green, and Felix Houston [sic], who carried the popular current against me.

In response to the charade, Lamar made it clear he intended to break up the camp.

I had an open rupture with Genl [sic] Rusk, believing it to be the secret arrangements of his to supplant me. Some hostile correspondence ensued; which instead of leading to further difficulty, has resulted in this arrangement, viz, that he is to recognize my orders in the future; that the regulars and about 6 or 8 volunteer companies are to march to another encampment under my command; where I shall issue my orders as Commander in Chief to the balance of the army of Texas, and if Green and Felix Houston [sic] still maintain their present attitude of rebellion to my authority, I shall punish them by Court Martial if possible, and if not shall report them to Congress. You will perceive from this dreadful state of affairs the high and absolute necessity of convening a Congress.

None of this happened.

In a postscript, Lamar added that he had received a letter from Rusk. It stated that the men were now refusing to follow Rusk, since the vote against Lamar affirmed his authority was neither valid nor constitutional.

In other words, the troops had decided that the army's commanders did not come from the government authority, and Rusk was clearly part of the government.

"Genl [sic] Rusk says he will now stand by me in defense of the Civil authority; he sees his own power departing as well as mine," Lamar wrote.

Lamar was not fooled. He saw the entire episode as Rusk's failed mission to consolidate his power among Houston supporters via a mutiny that he lost control of. In the end, he couldn't control the troops' fevered admiration and loyalty for Houston any more than Lamar.

[T]he whole has been produced by his desire for promotion, and finding that his new allies are not aiming at his support but at their own aggrandizement, he is willing to cooperate with me, but I fear that nothing that he can now do will be of any service in the cause of restoring that authority which his previous conduct has prostrated.

With that, Lamar withdrew from command. He said he intended to retire from public life.

That idea didn't last long.

"San Jacinto"

I.

"Come to the Bower," they sang,
Immortal spirits, crowned with flame,
On yonder heights of radiant bloom.
From freedom's deathless fields they came.
From mountain pass and prison gloom;
Dyed with the blood of Marathon,
Drenched with Salamis' bitter sea,
From where the sun of Leuctra shone,
And from thy rocks, Thermopylae.

"Come to the Bower," they sang,
The old Paladins cased in mail,
Whose standards sparkled to the morn,
And peers and princes from the vale
Where Roland blew his mighty horn;
And Scottish chiefs from Bannockburn,
And English knights from Ascalon,
And sturdy hearts whose memories turn
Toward Bunker Hill and Lexington.

"Come to the Bower," they sang,
"Come join our deathless throng and glow
Like us, while earth and heaven shall stand."
But yesterday the Alamo,
Unbroken, sent its glorious band,
And Goliad, from a reeking field,
Passed up her heroes! Crowned with flowers,
Behold us! Come with sword and shield,
And bask in fame's immortal bowers."

II.

By San Jacinto's placid stream
The warriors heard and, shining far,
They saw the splendid morning gleam
Of one imperial, changeless star;
They followed where its gleaming led:

To Hope, to Peace, to Victory,
For, from beneath her martyr dead,
Behold, a nation rose up free!

Lo! now around this hallowed stone
They press, the living and the dead,
And banners on the air are blown,
And quick and stirring orders sped;
Houston and Sherman, brave Lamar,
Millard and Hockley close around,
And, lo! with steady, swinging step,
A phantom sentry makes his round.

"Goliad! Alamo!" hark, the cry
Amid the rolling of the drums!
Hark, the Twin Sisters' hoarse reply
Upon the battle-breeze that comes!
Stand back! for rank and file press by
A-wearied, in the sunset's glow.
And in their midst they bear on high
The broken sword of Mexico!

Texas, thou queen of States, whose crown,
Wrought by the hands of heroes, shines
Like some prophetic sun adown
The glowing future's magic lines,
Arise, and, with imperial tread,
Draw near this consecrated place,
And bless thine own, thy mighty dead,
The saviors of thy glorious race!

—Mollie E. Moore Davis

PART II
POLITICAL WARS

7

PRESENT THE BATTLE SWORD

L ike Lamar, Houston wanted peace—at least for the moment.
Houston retired from public and military life after the revolution.
The republic moved on after the threat of a second Mexican invasion died
down. Thoughts turned to the first national election for a president.

Houston paid attention to the election but did not seek a candidacy.

"He wished to retire from public life, for he believed there would be
no necessity of firing another hostile gun in Texas, if the public councils
were guided by firmness and wisdom," wrote Charles Edward Lester in
a Houston biography. "He had been unrelentingly persecuted, and his
feelings outraged, just in proportion as he had devoted himself to the State.
In retirement, he could be happy, and his country free. He was, therefore,
disinclined to mingle in the turmoil of public life."

That is, until he wasn't.

Political success in the new republic was not based on governance skills or
even merit. Elections ran on personality and popularity.

The Stephen F. Austin Party and the John and William Wharton Party
emerged looking for candidates that could win the election. The two parties
accomplished much together at different times in the revolution. Now, they
saw themselves at odds.

Austin, as the empresario of the first Anglo-Texas colony, quickly captured
the title of the Father of Texas. When Santa Anna threw him into prison,
many considered it the match that lit the fire for the revolution.

The Austin Party used that milestone event to tag him for the presidency. That does not mean, however, that his supporters created the "Party of Austin."

What they created was better described as the Never Wharton Party, as Wooten noted.

> *The former was not strictly an Austin party, for all the people loved and revered Stephen F. Austin, but his immediate, personal friends felt that injustice had been done him on account of his position in regard to the war with Mexico and the early declaration of Texan independence, and that such injustice was largely due to the ambitious intrigues of John A. and William H. Wharton. Resentment against the Whartons produced personal opposition to them among Austin's closest followers, and it was an anti-Wharton rather than an Austin party.*

Meanwhile, the Wharton Party backed Henry Smith. He was the impeached governor of the rebel government. The party gained most of its followers from the reputation of Wharton rather than the candidate's.

Most people didn't pay attention to either party.

Instead, they paid attention to Houston.

Houston-mania was alive and well in early Texas, Wooten noted.

> *They had known but little of General Austin, as he had been absent in the United States since most of them came to the country, and his services as the real founder and father of Texas were not felt nor appreciated by them.*
>
> *To them General Houston was the central figure in the Revolution, whose success they considered had been won by his valor and skill, and as the "hero of San Jacinto" his military fame, as so often happens, outshone the less sensational achievements of civil life.*

As time went on, public meetings were held in Columbia, Nacogdoches, San Augustine and other Texas settlements. Houston's name was thrown about as a candidate at almost all of them. Burnet took notice of this.

In Burnet's effort to craft the election, he felt that Austin was the most likely candidate to become president. Burnet decided that the only reason Houston was being considered was because the army might try to stage a coup.

Houston had a reputation for being "a skilful [sic] politician, adroit, dramatic, popular in his speech and manner, and trained in a State where politics and public speaking had reached the position of a fine art," Wooten wrote.

Some believed Houston had become a candidate against his wishes and only agreed because the settlers reached a consensus on him.

Lester believed that Houston had become a candidate twelve days before the election because he was overcome with political concern for the future of the republic.

"The parties were pretty equally balanced, and there was great reason to fear that those out of power would so far embarrass the administration as to destroy its efficiency," Lester wrote. "He believed, that since he belonged to neither party, and possessed the confidence of the great mass of the people, he might still render signal service to the State, and he allowed his name to be used."

The Wharton Party dumped Smith. The brothers threw their support to Houston.

Houston became the first president of the Republic of Texas with a whopping 4,307 votes. Smith captured 745 votes, and Austin came up with only 587 votes.

Austin might have won if he had campaigned harder or spoken about working with Mexico earlier. He also might have won if he had handled the politics of Houston better.

In fact, it's possible to say that if Houston had a strong opponent, he might never have won.

Lamar, out of retirement and with Burnet's support, was elected vice-president. Wooten claimed he won because of the praises Houston gave him in his report on the Battle of San Jacinto.

Lamar captured the position with 2,699 votes, a landslide against his opponents.

The Installation Had a Level of Spite

The feuding began the minute Houston became president.

Before Houston's installation, Burnet's last major act as president of the rebel government was to call for a vote to ratify the constitution. The ballot also called for a vote on United States annexation if leaders arranged it. Voters were practically unanimous on each measure.

The voter-approved constitution made it clear when the transition of power had to occur. Houston and Lamar were scheduled to be installed in December 1836.

However, chatter and positioning to install Houston earlier began in October. Elected representatives began to clamor that Houston needed to be the president immediately. The fervor grew so strong that within the month, they'd won the argument.

On October 22, 1836, Burnet resigned. Within hours, congress passed a resolution to install Houston and Lamar at 4:00 p.m. the very same day.

A committee met Houston at that time and took him to the bar of the house of representatives. The speaker of the house proclaimed him president of the Republic of Texas that same minute.

Houston then delivered an extemporaneous speech. His supporters declared it was "the product of a great mind, a far-reaching statesman." He began with a flourish.

> *Mr. Speaker and Gentlemen: Deeply impressed with a sense of the responsibility devolving on me, I can not [sic], in justice to myself, repress the emotion of my heart, or restrain the feelings which my sense of obligation to my fellow citizens has inspired. Their suffrage was gratuitously bestowed. Preferred to others, not unlikely superior in merit to myself, called to the most important station among mankind by the voice of a free people, it is utterly impossible not to feel impressed with the deepest sensations of delicacy in my present position before the world.*

Houston believed that his opponents would have filled the cabinets with political friends. If that happened, the republic would always have a chaotic, penniless government, Lester wrote. Houston's speech alluded to that underneath his glamorous, over-the-top rhetoric.

> *It is not here alone, but our present attitude before all nations has rendered my position, and that of my country, one of peculiar interest. A spot of earth almost unknown to the geography of the age, destitute of all available resources, few in numbers, we remonstrated against oppression, and, when invaded by a numerous host, we dared to proclaim our independence and to strike for freedom on the breast of the oppressor. As yet our course is on ward. We are only in the outset of the campaign of liberty. Futurity has locked up the destiny which awaits our people. Who can contemplate with apathy a situation so imposing in the moral and physical world? No one. The relations among ourselves are peculiarly delicate and important; for no matter what zeal or fidelity I may possess in the discharge of my official duties, if I do not obtain co-operation and an honest support from*

the co-ordinate departments of the government, wreck and ruin must be the inevitable consequences of my administration.

Houston implored his legislation to keep him under control. He considered the respite of war to be more comfortable than politics. Houston's references to the glories of the revolution filtered through most of his speech. It worked, because many legislators had also served under his command.

If, then, in the discharge of my duty, my competency should fail in the attainment of the great objects in view, it would become your sacred duty to correct my errors and sustain me by your superior wisdom. This much I anticipate—this much I demand. I am perfectly aware of the difficulties that surround me, and the convulsive throes through which our country must pass. I have never been emulous of the civic wreath—when merited, it crowns a happy destiny. A country situated like ours is environed with difficulties, its administration is fraught with perplexities. Had it been my destiny, I would infinitely have preferred the toils, privations, and perils of a soldier, to the duties of my present station. Nothing but zeal, stimulated by the holy spirit of patriotism, and guided by philosophy and reason, can give that impetus to our energies necessary to surmount the difficulties that obstruct our political progress.

Eventually, Houston addressed the complexities of starting a new republic. He made clear that he supported treaties of peace with the Native Americans. He believed that they could live together for mutual benefit inside the republic.

He never wavered from that vision. He held to it even when it was known Mexico used the Cherokees, Caddos and Cushattas to conduct massacres in San Antonio, Goliad and San Jacinto.

During the revolution, Burnet asked the United States to intervene. The rebel government hoped the "neutral" government could intervene in Mexico's mercenary scheme. Houston also negotiated a treaty to try to manage the problem.

As a result, the United States stationed troops near Louisiana to battle the Native Americans.

A subject of no small importance is the situation of an extensive frontier, bordered by Indians, and open to their depredation. Treaties of peace and amity, and the maintenance of good faith with the Indians, seem to me the most rational means for winning their friendship. Let us abstain from aggression, establish commerce with the different tribes, supply their useful and necessary wants, maintain even-handed justice with them, and natural reason will teach them the utility of our friendship.

Nonetheless, Houston believed maintaining a strong military was one way to keep the peace.

Admonished by the past, we can not [sic], in justice, disregard our national enemies. Vigilance will apprise us of their approach, a disciplined and valiant army will insure their discomfiture. Without discrimination and system, how unavailing would all the resources of an old and overflowing treasury prove to us. It would be as unprofitable to us in our present situation as the rich diamond locked in the bosom of the adamant. We can not [sic] hope that the bosom of our beautiful prairies will soon be visited by the healing breezes of peace. We may again look for the day when their verdure will be converted into dyes of crimson. We must keep all our energies alive, our army organized, disciplined, and increased to our present emergencies. With these preparations we can meet and vanquish despotic thousands. This is the attitude we at present must regard as our own. We are battling for human liberty; reason and firmness must characterize our acts.

Houston, in stark contrast to the graciousness he gave Santa Anna, had fighting words for Mexico. He peppered them with religious nationalism and racial superiority.

[W]e were hunted down as the felon wolf, our little band driven from fastness to fastness, exasperated to the last extreme; while the blood of our kindred and our friends invoking the vengeance of an offended God was smoking to high heaven, we met our enemy and vanquished them. They fell in battle, or suppliantly kneeled and were spared. We offered up our vengeance at the shrine of humanity, while Christianity rejoiced at the act and looked with pride on the sacrifice. The civilized world contemplated with proud emotions conduct which reflected so much glory on the Anglo-Saxon race. The moral effect has done more to wards [sic] our liberation than the defeat of the army of veterans.

Describing the friends of the republic, Houston pointed to William Christy of Louisiana. Christy sat inside the legislative bar by invitation. He had been a funding source and ardent supporter of Texas independence from his home state.

> *Where our cause has been presented to our friends in the land of our origin, they have embraced it with their warmest sympathies. They have rendered us manly and efficient aids. They have rallied to our standard, they have fought side by side with our warriors. They have bled, and their dust is mingling with the ashes of our heroes. At this moment I discern numbers around me who battled in the field of San Jacinto, and whose chivalry and valor have identified them with the glory of the country, its name, its soil, and its liberty. There sits a gentleman within my view whose personal and political services to Texas have been invaluable. He was the first in the United States to respond to our cause. His purse was ever open to our necessities. His hand was extended in our aid. His presence among us and his return to the embraces of our friends will inspire new efforts on behalf of our cause.*

And finally, Houston addressed the voter mandate for annexation. He called the United States the "Republican family in the North."

> *A circumstance of the highest import will claim the attention of the court at Washington. In our recent election the important subject of annexation to the United States of America was submitted to the consideration of the people. They have expressed their feelings and their wishes on that momentous subject. They have, with a unanimity unparalleled, declared that they will be reunited to the great Republican family of the North. The appeal is made by a willing people. Will our friends disregard it? They have already bestowed upon us their warmest sympathies. Their manly and generous feelings have been enlisted on our behalf. We are cheered by the hope that they will receive us to participate in their civil, political, and religious rights, and hail us welcome into the great family of freemen. Our misfortunes have been their misfortunes—our sorrows, too, have been theirs, and their joy at our success has been irrepressible.*

Houston then presented his battle sword. As he stretched it out, several in the audience rushed him, overcome with the heat of his emotional display.

> *I have worn it with some humble pretensions in defence [sic] of my country, and should the danger of my country again call for my services, I expect to resume it, and respond to that call, if needful, with my blood and my life.*

81

With that, Houston, battle sword in hand, became the first president of the Republic of Texas.

8

HOUSTON ON DISPLAY

With less drama than Houston, Lamar, as vice-president, delivered his inaugural address to both houses of congress. He addressed the senate the next day. His speeches were the complete opposite of Houston's, which were rousing in nature.

That didn't mean Lamar wasn't steaming inside. He later wrote in his diary that he believed Houston had manipulated the entire installation.

> *Houston was so anxious to enter upon the duties of his office, that Burnet was forced by the threats of members of Congress that if he did not retire for the new President he would be pushed out. The Constitutional period for the installation of the President had not arrived as yet by a month. Houston could not wait. Burnet was forced to retire. Austin advised him to do it for the sake of peace; and insinuated that if he did not Congress would probably push him out. This was the first act of the government, a palpable violation of the Constitution. That little month Houston could not wait; nor could the hungry expectants brook the delay who were looking forward to presidential favors.*

While Lamar may have gained a stellar reputation as a gentleman, he was not above playing politics. His power move was his involvement in creating a thirty-eight-page pamphlet that embedded itself into Texas politics.

Lamar owned the printing press that Algernon P. Thompson used to publish the *Velasco Herald*. Almost no one knew that the prolific poet owned the equipment.

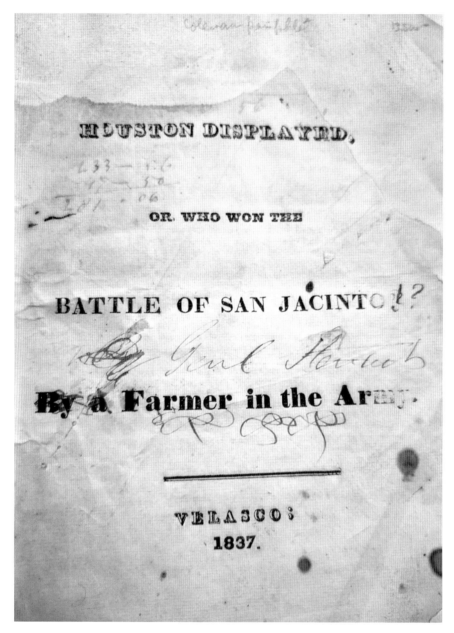

The cover of *Houston Displayed*, which Lamar had secretly printed to discredit Houston during his first administration as the president of the republic. *Courtesy of the Bryan Museum.*

In 1837, this printing press was used to print, publish and distribute *Houston Displayed: Or, Who Won the Battle of San Jacinto.*

The anti-Houston factions were fresh with anger over Houston's policies and his battlefield decisions. They looked for ways to undermine him.

They pegged the quiet yet fierce Robert M. Coleman, who had been an aide-de-camp to Houston at the Battle of San Jacinto.

BRUTAL METHODS

Post revolution, Coleman had a band of soldiers who operated under the direction of Burnet. They worked around the region surrounding present-day Bastrop. Coleman used hawk approaches to confront the Native Americans west of the Colorado River.

Their methods could be as brutal as those they fought. One account stated that after a vicious battle, Coleman and his troops captured seven warriors.

Coleman ignored the protests from some of his troops to let the prisoners live. He and several members, instead, violently killed and scalped them. One member even scalped a warrior's back.

Working the front line in the Anglo–Native American battles, Coleman was furious that Houston would want peace with the ferocious warriors he dealt with daily.

Houston, before he was president, did not agree with Coleman's actions and wrote him to that effect. In the same letter, he announced the new official policy with Native Americans would be one of peace.

The letter astonished Coleman, who had been expanding the defense northwest of present-day Bastrop. He moved troops into new stations and gave them orders to survey and scout new sectors.

Coleman wrote Burnet that he challenged anyone to investigate his official actions to protect the frontier settlers. He was not going to stand down. He implored Burnet to help him find ways to continue his work.

Coleman's letter arrived after October 22, 1836. Burnet had already resigned, and Houston was president.

While Burnet and Lamar seethed at Houston's maneuver to gain power, someone approached the incredulous Coleman, and *Houston Displayed* appeared.

In the pamphlet, Coleman presents an expansive account of Houston's actions between October 1835 and April 1836.

Coleman used Thompson (and perhaps one of the Whartons) as the pamphlet's ghostwriter. Interestingly, Coleman does not appear as the author. The pamphlet says it was written "by a Farmer in the Army," but Coleman was always known as the author.

In fact, over time, the publication became known simply as "Coleman's Pamphlet."

Coleman reviewed his past with Houston. He claimed his desire to print the pamphlet was to speak the truth about what he knew. The author states that if Mexico wanted a second invasion, Houston was not fit to lead the army, even if he said he was.

Using this premise, Coleman gave a tell-all that unleashed every misdeed and mistake he considered Houston to have made. The new president would not escape these accusations for the rest of his life.

Coleman takes aim at Houston from the first pages. He casually mentions that Houston may or may not have been a Mexican sympathizer. He infers that Houston may have wanted to see Stephen F. Austin fail.

Coleman ridicules Houston's treaty with Native Americans and his efforts to remain neutral in the revolution. This treaty aimed to keep Native Americans from becoming Mexican mercenaries. Houston's relationship with the Native Americans is a critical thread throughout the pamphlet.

Coleman claims that Houston was jealous of Fannin. He charges that Houston feared Fannin wanted to be commander-in-chief. The farmer questions whether Houston supported Fannin at all. Using Fannin's final letters to the rebel government as evidence, Coleman charges that Houston had let Fannin and his troops die.

Can it be possible that, in this hour of danger, the Commander-in-Chief was not at his post? Yes, it is a notorious fact, that during the latter part of the fall and the whole winter, when the enemy was making preparations to invade us, the Commander-in-Chief spent his time electioneering for civil office, and scouting among the Cherokees; which savages he had made his equals by long and familiarly associating with them; treating away lands that actually belonged to the citizens of Texas. He brought with him to the Convention for the ratification of that body his favorite Indian treaty; and declared, publicly, that the salvation of the country depended upon its ratification.

THE FIRST ACCOUNT OF HOUSTON'S DRUNKENNESS

One of the most damning tales from Coleman is a firsthand account of Houston's prolific drunkenness. Coleman remembered being in the council room at San Felipe about half past midnight. Thompson entered and said he should "see the condition of your Commander-in-Chief."

Coleman went to the grog shop (or saloon) and saw a mess of twenty drunken men and a passed-out violin player. Houston was near the fireplace, where two people were holding him up. He proclaimed the many Napoleonic feats that awaited Texas on the battlefield.

> *The harangue was of course received with loud cheers, clapping of hands and other elegant expressions of approbation, which awoke the old man with the violin, who paid his compliments by drawing his bow a few times across the strings and resuming his sleep. After order was restored, some person gave a general invitation to drink but alas on the first motion of the General, the union was dissolved; the two pillars that supported it fell, one to the right, the other to the left, and the center measured its length exactly in front. I returned to my room in a state of despondency; is it possible, said I, that such is the conduct of the Commander-in-Chief of the Texian Army, to who hands the defence [sic] of the country is confided? If so, Texas, without a miracle must be lost.*

In quick order, Coleman said the townspeople sent Houston to Gonzalez to command the troops. When Houston left, he claimed he had been drunk for five years but, on that particular day, was sober. He refused a drink and inhaled smelling salts instead.

Then Coleman claimed that when Houston arrived in Gonzalez, he didn't lead with confidence or a steady hand. Instead, Coleman charged that Houston had moments that swung between madness and dejectedness.

It was during a moment of Houston's madness that he ordered Gonzalez be burned in a quick retreat. His decision to order the burnings of towns gave Santa Anna precedence to do the same. Coleman charged Houston with the destruction of settlements.

This instability, Coleman declared, made the men disorganized. Houston was a lousy leader, a coward and the creator of the Runway Scrape. His decisions left widows and children defenseless after the fall of the Alamo.

The acts of mutiny began in earnest after Houston's retreat at Groce's, according to the pamphlet. Coleman recalled an event when Houston learned that one of his majors had written a letter to Burnet about his mood swings.

This letter also stated he had a drinking problem, an opiate addiction and a smelling salt addiction. Houston found the letter, opened it and confronted the major. The subordinate said to Houston, "I love my General but my country better."

After that, Coleman said, Houston turned his wrath on the major and became a bitter enemy.

Many of the allegations Coleman wrote about were already documented or levied by other troop members. The power of *Houston Displayed* was that they were now in one location. They were contained in a pamphlet small enough to fit in a pocket.

WHO WON THE BATTLE?

As an aide-de-camp, Coleman's position with Houston at San Jacinto gave him a unique perspective. He had moments with the commander that others were never privy to.

One of his criticisms of Houston starts with Sherman's skirmish on the battlefield. Coleman stated that he believed Sherman had failed and that a person had died because Houston did not back up Sherman quickly enough. In fact, Coleman claimed Houston was hidden from the troops when Sherman's plan went awry.

> *I do believe that when Gen. Houston first drew out his men, it was with a determination to fight; but from some cause he changed his mind; of which change he ought earlier to have informed Col. Sherman, and not have remained silent until that gallant officer had engaged the enemy and gained such an advantage....The intention of the General, on this day, is unknown, I presume, to all. Shadows, clouds, and the darkness of mystery hang over it.*

Eventually, Coleman charged that Houston wanted to expose Colonel Sherman to dangerous situations so he would die.

Before the Battle of San Jacinto, Coleman stated that Wharton pushed a reluctant Houston to fight. In Coleman's account, Houston fitted the council of war with cronies whom he knew would advocate for a retreat.

Coleman said the troops countered Houston. They used Wharton as a spokesperson to convince Houston they had no interest in a retreat. Coleman's pamphlet claimed Houston told Wharton that the men would not fight, but Wharton debated him.

Coleman wrote, "'The officers will fight,' said Wharton, 'and are now anxiously awaiting orders, which I will instantly give, unless you give a special order to the contrary.'"

Houston never issued a special order. Coleman charged that Wharton ordered the "whole camp to prepare for battle" and then formed the attack for the upcoming battle.

A critical moment in Coleman's recount comes shortly after he reveals Houston told Colonel Henry Millard the Mexican reinforcements had arrived. Millard commanded the company that ran through the Mexican breastwork, a critical moment in the battle. When Houston was shot, Coleman claimed he cried, "By G-d [sic] the reinforcements have arrived, Cos has come up, I'm killed, and all is lost!"

Coleman claimed that as Houston said this, the troops broke the Mexican ranks and Santa Anna's troops began scattering. Coleman claimed Houston, in that moment, ordered a halt to stop the fighting. Then Wharton arrived to tell him Sherman had engaged the Mexicans just out of sight.

Houston didn't believe him, and Colonel Rusk had to be brought in to confirm the report. Houston still didn't believe either of them, which Coleman said was a "pretended disbelief."

At that point, Coleman said the troops started cheering for Rusk and Wharton to take over the battle and command them.

Coleman, in his final words on the battle, said that when he brought the prisoners to Houston, he was rebuffed and insulted. He wrote that he believed he and others had done good work to bring honor to the Texian name, and Houston didn't care.

THE HOUSTON WRATH

Houston did not take the pamphlet and its effective distribution lightly. William Wharton used it as the basis for a Houston impeachment, which didn't happen.

Houston turned his attention to Coleman, who soon felt the "Houston wrath" the pamphlet detailed.

In February 1837, one of Coleman's troops tied a drunken ranger to a tree, where he choked to death. Instead of jailing the troop member, Houston jailed Coleman in Velasco.

Houston then made Coleman sit in jail without any charges or a bail hearing.

A few days later, reports emerged that Houston had gloated about his scheme to get revenge. In a letter to frontier settler Daniel Parker, Houston wrote:

> *Your favor has reached me, and no man can regret more sincerely than I do the misfortune that has taken place.…They now see how matters are to be.…If men will not obey orders, they will find that another power, is at least equal to disobedience. This power I will exercise!*

For three months, Coleman remained in jail. Eventually, Chief Justice James Collinsworth in Brazoria heard about the situation. He ordered Houston to release Coleman. Houston released him, and his former aide-de-camp promptly died.

Coleman drowned when his boat capsized near Velasco.

The fallout from Coleman's pamphlet lived on. The United States had copies of it. The *New Orleans True American* questioned Houston's Louisiana doctor, Ashbel Smith, "as to the truth about President Houston's conduct, his drinking, his beastliness, and his generally erratic behavior."

Exactly a year after the pamphlet's distribution, the *Texas Telegraph*, on February 24, 1838, printed Smith's response. It read, in part:

> *As regards his mind, he is still in the pride of his intellect.…*[H]*is bearing is that of the most lofty and princely courtesy.…Despite what has been said to the contrary, I believe him to be the most popular man in Texas. The statements of him being a madman and cutting tall antics before high Heaven and man are utterly and gratuitously false.*

For the rest of his life, Houston never trusted anyone associated with Coleman's pamphlet.

9

CAPITAL OF CHAOS

The republic attracted a run of reckless and ambitious people. Greedy frauds and antigovernment self-interested pioneers flocked to the republic. When they couldn't find a way into the government, they joined the army, which had moved from Victoria to Lavaca.

These pioneers joined as volunteers and spent a good deal of time concocting mutiny. Reports stated that the military had become a den for the wild and lawless. The military itself had become a threat to civil authority. Lamar saw the extent himself at Victoria.

The troops also had demands. One of them was the continuing call for the death of Santa Anna. The other was the resurrection of the Matamoros Campaign that Fannin was commanding when Santa Anna had him killed.

The unruly troops had confounded Houston again.

Houston's troops had a penchant for allowing murders to occur after the men had drunk themselves into wild and violent rages. Houston, meanwhile, had also become a problem, because he would challenge men to duels that didn't end well.

During this time, the archives of the new republic were put in a trunk and locked. They went to Columbia. Then the new administration began the long process of starting a new government.

With the army's demands looming large over Santa Anna, Houston turned his attention toward him. The Mexican general had been imprisoned in Orozimbo (present-day Angleton) a few miles from Columbia. About twenty men who oversaw his custody had mistreated him and been violent toward him.

A replica of the original Republic of Texas capitol building in Columbia. *Author's collection; from the public domain.*

The abuse left Santa Anna of no use to the republic at all. The broken general had come to believe that he would be a prisoner for the rest of his life. He never expected to speak to Houston again. But he was wrong.

Before he became president, Houston brought a group of his supporters to meet with Santa Anna. The meeting became emotional. The men cried together. Houston's supporters said he cried at the state Santa Anna had been reduced to in prison. Santa Anna cried at the loss of his dignity.

Santa Anna told Houston that he'd written President Jackson. Houston promised Santa Anna to intervene with Jackson when he became president. Then Christy and others in Houston's party gave Santa Anna gifts to comfort him. They ate together.

Later, Houston attempted to have Santa Anna released from prison. Congress refused. The leaders even met in secret to create a resolution to have the Mexican general executed. Houston vetoed it.

The senate only agreed to his release after Houston pleaded again that an execution would ruin the future of Texas.

With that settled, Houston sent escorts to take Santa Anna to visit President Jackson. When they began their journey with the former general, the escorts got lost on their way to the Sabine River. They detoured through San Jacinto.

Their reports stated that Santa Anna became overwhelmed when he saw the bones of his troops on the field. He stopped as the escorts continued to ride. When they realized he was not behind them, they retraced their steps to find him. When they found him, he was reflecting on the battlefield. They gathered him in silence and continued the journey.

After the meeting in Washington, Jackson sent Santa Anna back to Mexico on a war vessel. He soon reestablished himself as the country's leader.

A Mighty Bad Place for a Capital

The capitol building of Texas, where Houston had become the president, was an unassuming clapboard building in Columbia. After Houston's inauguration, the First Congress met there.

Because the accommodations were poor, congress and Houston wanted to move the capital. At that moment, two brothers, A.C. and John K. Allen, founded a new town at the head of Buffalo Bayou.

They called it, interestingly, Houston.

With a narrow vote in both houses, congress adopted an act to temporarily locate the capital in Houston City. The act said the capital could be moved again at the end of the congressional session in 1840.

CAPITOL BUILDING AT HOUSTON, 1837.

Houston's capitol building. *Author's collection; from the public domain.*

The move to Houston's namesake city was not a godsend by any means. The place had no houses. Its streets were bad. The town was basically unhealthy—and those were the easy problems.

The First Congress had to convene on the promise that there would be enough room for each member by its second meeting on May 1, 1837. That promise didn't come to fruition.

The matter of the Houston City capital was so controversial that it became an election issue for congress by August 9, 1837, just a few months later.

When the First Congress met in the fall, its members appointed a committee to find a permanent capital. They were to find a place "located between the Guadalupe and Trinity Rivers, not more than one hundred miles north of the upper San Antonio Road, nor south of a line from the Trinity to the Guadalupe, crossing the Brazos at Fort Bend."

Congress still, however, had three more miserable years in Houston City.

Lamar's Victory Lap

Houston's wrath over the publication of the *Houston Displayed* pamphlet was well known. While the knowledge of Lamar's involvement as the printing press owner never made it to the mainstream, Lamar made an interesting decision when the scandal hit.

He wanted to return to his native Georgia during his term as vice-president.

When Congress adjourned, he asked and received leave to focus on the topics he dreamed of when he first arrived in Texas. He spent months collecting materials about the history of Texas and traveled around the republic documenting the stories of the original settlers.

Then instead of presiding over the second session of congress in May 1837, Lamar returned to Georgia. The Georgia public showered him with attention and celebration. Stephen H. Evritt acted as the vice-president in his absence.

Lamar's victory lap was interrupted, however, when Richard Royall, a revolutionary donor and a friend of Burnet, wrote the vice-president to return home. Royall wanted him to begin campaigning for the presidency.

Royall wrote that Houston talked often about quitting. The president had been drinking and gambling and had become generally incompetent.

RESIDENCE OF PRESIDENT HOUSTON, 1836
(while the capitol was being built).

Houston's cabin in Houston City, circa 1836. *Courtesy of the Texas State Library and Archives Commission.*

Lamar ignored the letter. He continued his road tour until the Texas Senate, in a secret session, adopted a resolution in September 1837. It instructed Evritt to write Lamar about the issues they were facing.

> *The approach of the season when movement by our nation's enemy may be looked for, the opening of the land office for the distribution of the public domain, which is presumed will soon take place, and the protracted illness of his Excellency the President, presents a crisis in our affairs that devolves unusual responsibility on our Government. The safety of the country requires her leaders to take their posts.*
>
> *Your presence is wanted in her Councils, your arms may be needed for her defence* [sic].

The letter and resolution were enough to capture the vice-president's attention. Lamar returned in November 1837 and never received any fallout from his role as the distributor of *Houston Displayed*.

In December, a virtually unanimous congress asked Lamar to run for the presidency.

> *In our anxiety to select the most suitable person to fill the office of President of this Republic, at the expiration of the term of General Sam Houston, we are satisfied from a knowledge of your character civil and military that you would be his most appropriate successor. We respectfully request that you would inform us if you will permit your name to be used as a candidate for that high office. In making this request we are confident and happy in the belief that we express the wishes of a large majority of our fellow citizens.*

Lamar did not accept his candidacy right away. He heard Rusk, who had undermined him with a mutiny at Victoria, was also being considered. Lamar wrote to him to arrange a meeting to discuss how to handle the situation.

> *I have just received a letter, from several distinguished gentlemen, our mutual friends inviting me [to] become a candidate for the next Presidency. As you have been spoken of frequently for the same high office I am anxious to see you before I give a final answer. It is important that harmony at all times should be preserved in our country and at the present period any violent contest for the Chief Magistry could not fail to be extremely prejudicial to the peace and prosperity of the country, but might prove fatal to its best hopes.*
>
> *I know that you as well as myself must deprecate these consequences, and with a view to avoid them, I think it all important that we should have a free and unreserved conference and by comparing our views come to some conclusion which whilst it may be satisfactory to ourselves will be most conducive to public interest. I shall be at my room at about 2 o'clock, when I hope it will be convenient for you to call upon me.*

Amazingly, Rusk conceded without a meeting.

> *Your note of this morning has been received informing me of a request having been made by several distinguished gentlemen to you to become a candidate for the Presidency of the Republic at the next election and desiring a free and unreserved conference between us on that subject before you answer their communication.*
>
> *I fully subscribe to the propriety of the course you suggest and am proud to say that it gives me another proof in addition to the many I have already had of your patriotism and desire to promote the harmony and good of the country.*

From a press of business it will not be in my power to call at your room at 2 o'clock this evening but I hope you will not on my account have any hesitancy in giving your consent to the request alluded to as there is no design or desire on my part to have my name before the people for any office whatever.

As the representative of my country I feel bound to discharge to the best of my abilities the duties of the Station; but beyond this my private affairs and domestic obligations so long neglected imperiously demand my attention and will not permit me to think of public life beyond the discharge of those military obligations in the hour of danger which I hold paramount to all other considerations. But I shall be pleased, dear sir, to see your name before the people for the office of Chief Magistrate and shall be happy to sustain you in your labors for the welfare of the country to which we are both under many obligations for confidence reposed and honors conferred.

With that, Lamar accepted the nomination for the presidency. The mutiny at Victoria was never again an issue.

The Bizarre, Bitter Election of 1838

The towns west of the Trinity River clamored to nominate Lamar for the presidency as quickly as they had clamored for Houston in the previous election.

The defection made Houston unhappy. Because, by law, he was not allowed to run for a second consecutive term, he began to seek someone who could beat Lamar.

That proved more difficult than one would think.

The Houston Party first supported Peter W. Grayson, who had an accomplished résumé. He had been Houston's attorney general until he became an annexation commissioner for the United States. After that, he became Houston's naval agent.

A professional lawyer, he was a confidant of Stephen F. Austin and a respected troop who served in the revolution with him. When Austin was imprisoned in Mexico, Grayson was among those who traveled to secure his release.

Grayson also had a history of mental health problems that plagued him through the years. He found some respite in the 1820s, but after he was nominated for the presidency, it returned in fervor.

At the time of Grayson's nomination, he was a minister plenipotentiary (a type of ambassador) for Texas to the United States. He left that position to run for the presidency. He also asked a woman in Tennessee, whom he had courted for a long time, to marry him. She declined.

The race was difficult for him. He became despondent after facing a bitter misinformation campaign launched against him. When he stopped near Knoxville, Tennessee, on his trip to Washington, he wrote about the "terrible mental fiend that possessed me." He wrote that he was not happy with the presidential campaign. Many at the time suspected the jilted proposal also consumed his thoughts.

The morning after he wrote the letter, he fatally shot himself.

Candidate Number Two

James Collingsworth. *Courtesy of the Texas State Library and Archives Commission.*

The Houston Party searched again and found James Collinsworth, the first chief justice of the Republic of Texas, to become the second nominee. He had also served at San Jacinto and was the judge who ordered Houston to release Coleman from jail.

A pro-Houston supporter and a friend of President Jackson, Collinsworth was an ambassador to Washington on annexation. Like Grayson, Collinsworth had an impressive list of accomplishments. Rusk had commended him for his bravery and courage at the Battle of San Jacinto.

In a bit of irony, Houston had offered Collinsworth the attorney general position earlier. He declined it, so it went to Grayson.

The week of his nomination, Collinsworth was in a drunken stupor in Galveston. Later, he got on a steamboat, went overboard and died in Galveston Bay. Most reports claimed that people believed he died by suicide. Others claimed it was an accidental fall.

When his body was recovered, his friends had it sailed to Buffalo Bayou, where it lay in state at the Houston City Capitol. His funeral at City Cemetery was the first Masonic burial in Texas.

BELOW THE BELT POLITICS AND A MEDIA WAR

After the deaths of its two prior candidates, the Houston Party nominated Robert Wilson, who did not die.

The election was bitter on all fronts. The Houston Party levied deep misinformation campaigns, below-the-belt politics and a media war against Lamar.

The *Galveston Civilian* hated Lamar. Its editors claimed he was partially insane.

The *Telegraph and Texas Register* responded: "[W]e sincerely regret that his disorder is not contagious, in order that the country might reap some benefit from it even before election."

Opponents claimed Lamar was ineligible for election because he had not been a Texas citizen for three years. He replied that it was strange to accuse him of that after all his public service. He provided affidavits that showed he announced his intention to become a citizen in 1835.

On election day, Lamar trounced Wilson 6,995 to 252. Burnet, who was the president of the rebel government, was also easily elected as vice-president of the Republic of Texas. Burnet ran on the Lamar ticket. He captured 776 votes, which was a clear majority against his opponents, A.C. Horton and Joseph Rowe.

After Houston hijacked Lamar's inauguration with an emotional speech that left him weeping at his own words, the second president of the Republic of Texas immediately began his efforts to overturn each of Houston's initiatives.

First, Lamar wanted a Texas nation with mutual trade partners throughout the world. He wasn't going to send anyone else to Washington to talk about annexation. He hoped for recognition of Texan independence by European governments. He sought a favorable commercial treaty with the United States.

> *If we will but maintain our present independent position—diffuse knowledge and virtue by means of public education—establish a sound and wholesome monetary system—remove the temptation and facilities to every species of peculation and unrighteous gain make truth, virtue and patriotism the basis of all public policy—and secure the confidence of foreign nations by the wisdom of our laws and the integrity of our motives, I cannot perceive why we may not, within a very short period, elevate our young republic into that political importance and proud distinction which*

will not only command the respect and admiration of the world, but render it the interest of the nations now discarding our friendship, to covet from us those commercial relations which we vainly solicit from them.

Lamar wasted no time establishing a public school system and university. He wanted a uniform municipal code. He supported English law over Spanish law and declared he wanted the Common Law of England by Statute. He supported free trade and a national bank.

More glaring, he completely opposed Houston's policy toward the Native Americans and wanted to begin an aggressive hard-nose stance against them.

He also supported getting the seat of government out of that disgustingly unaccommodating town named after Houston.

He wasted no time in getting that initiative started.

10

THE BUFFALO HUNT

Congressional leaders became irritated with the accommodation in Houston City and made it clear they wanted to move Texas's capital. Houston was not pleased.

In response to the action, Houston agreed to a vote on October 19, 1837. If approved, a committee of five commissioners would look for a permanent seat of government. It passed.

The commissioners were careful not to appear unethical, Crane wrote.

> *They had given public notice of their appointments so they could receive propositions for the "the sale of lands as may be made them, not less than one, nor more than six leagues of land; and also examine such places as they may think proper on vacant lands; and that they be authorized to enter into conditional contracts for the purchase of such locations as they may think proper, subject to ratification or rejection by this congress."*

The commissioners reported their findings in November 1837. Congress received and accepted their report. On March 8, 1838, congress appointed a real estate committee.

This committee had the power to negotiate a contract with John Eblin for the purchase of his league of land on the east bank of the Colorado River below La Grange.

The committee also had the power to reserve for the government all the vacant lands that were in a nine-mile radius of the western boundary of Eblin's league.

On April 14, 1838, the committee told congress that they had finished the purchase. On May 7, 1838, they reported the same to a joint committee of the two houses.

Two days later, congress voted to accept Eblin's league and drew up a bill to reflect the decision.

Houston vetoed the bill. He said the town named after him should remain the capital until 1840, as the First Congress had declared.

That's when the battle for the Texas capital began.

East and West Divide

The east and west sectors of Texas were divided by the Colorado River. Lamar was always supported by the west settlers. Houston was always supported by the east settlers.

This divide was so acrimonious that Lamar's followers in the east begged him to conduct his campaign in the west. It had a better chance of becoming successful over there. He followed that advice.

Houston came under fire from the west because the people there considered his veto to be a sign that he wanted a capital on his side of the Colorado River.

There was also the argument that he had an ego and liked having the capital in a town named after him.

Grayson, the ill-fated Lamar presidential opponent, had agreed to keep the capital in the east. But with his death, the strongest candidate to make the case for a capital in Houston City was gone.

The *Matagorda Bulletin* supported a western capital and began a campaign to promote it. The editors claimed settlers had moved into the interior of Texas quickly after the revolution ended. It was a rapidly growing region. On March 7, 1838—the day the committee made its final report to the congress joint committee—the following appeared:

> *Several of our citizens have just returned from the up-country and the far West, where they have been engaged since the opening of the land office, in locating their lands. They bring the most flattering accounts of the emigration which is now pouring into the interior, with a rapidity altogether unparalleled in the settlement of the country. The new comers [sic] we understand are nearly all farmers, and are now making extensive*

preparations to cultivate the soil. The Colorado, up to the base of the
mountains, is alive with the opening of new plantations, and towns and
villages seem to be springing up spontaneously along its banks.

Two weeks later, the newspaper said Lamar was the best person to handle
the interior emigration. Emigration had suddenly become a top issue for the
next president.

But above all, the character and qualifications of the next chief magistrate
of the Republic of Texas, should be extensively and favourably known, to
the people of the United States. Emigration, which is so earnestly desired
by every good and patriotic citizen, and which alone can hasten the rising
greatness of this flourishing republic, will be checked or promoted by the
character of the man whom we shall elevate to that distinguished office.

The issue of a west capital remained a hot topic for the *Matagorda Bulletin*
in August 1837. Editors made the argument that a west capital would be
critical to building Texas's political and economic strength. It noted that
the capital

will be permanently located during the next two years; and no measure can
be so big with consequences to the West, and particularly to the citizens
of this Senatorial District as its location on the Colorado. It will promote
emigration to the West, thereby giving protection to the frontier settlements,
and enhancing the value of our lands. It will also increase most rapidly
the settlement of the lands of the Colorado, and of the country west of it,
thereby increasing the capital and interest of that section of the country,
which will result in important public improvements, increasing the facilities
of commerce and trade.

When Lamar became president, the issue was settled. On January 14,
1839, congress passed an act that solidified the capital in the west. Congress
selected a committee to find a place between the Trinity and Colorado
Rivers north of San Antonio Road.

The committee would need to find between one and four acres for sale
and seek to purchase the land under the public domain. If they could
not, they were allowed to buy it for no more than $3 per acre and a bond
of $1,000.

The Legend

A story was once told in Old Texas that if not for a buffalo hunt, the site chosen for Texas capital may never have been found. While this may or may not be true, the tale demonstrated Lamar's vision for an Anglo-American Texas empire.

The tale stated that Lamar had grown weary of the Houston administration between 1837 and 1838. Seeking respite, he and six friends headed to the site of the old Fort Prairie on the upper Colorado River.

The night before they arrived, they camped with Jacob Harrell, the only person who lived in one section of the trail. Native Americans so often attacked his homestead that he had a stockade made of split logs to protect his livestock and horses. His cabin sat on the banks of Shoal Creek near the river ford.

The next morning, Harrell's son awoke everyone with screams that the prairie was full of buffalo. Lamar and his company immediately killed all the buffalo they could. Afterward, a bugler called to them from behind on a hill. They walked up to it to meet him.

When Lamar looked down, he saw "a valley filled with wild rye, mountains up the river and a beautiful view of the south."

His friends stated that he said, "This should be the site of a future Empire."

When Lamar became president, he told the search committee to look at the hill he'd climbed. The committee chose a location that included the hill. They claimed this was because it provided natural defenses from the Native Americans.

They also said they thought trade with Sante Fe would be better created along the Colorado River than along the Brazos River, which had been their second choice.

Under Lamar's administration, the government hoped to build trade routes with Santa Fe, Matamoros, the Red River and the Texas seaports. They wanted all those routes to converge in one place. The report stated:

> In reference to the protection to be afforded to the frontier by the location of the Seat of Government, a majority of the Commissioners are of the opinion that that object will be as well attained by the location upon one river as upon the other, being also of the opinion that within a short period of time following the location of the Seat of Government on the Frontier, the extension of the Settlements produced thereby, will engender other theories of defence [sic], on lands now the homes of the Comanche and the Bison.

The site on the fabled hill would become the location of the Texas Capitol.

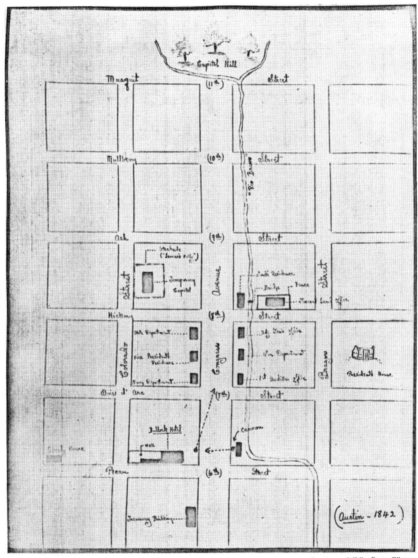

Austin at the time of the Archive War

Courtesy of Effie Dean Giles

The city layout of Austin in 1840 at the time of the Archive War. *Courtesy of the Briscoe Center for American History, University of Texas at Austin.*

ARRIVAL AT WATERLOO

Edward Burleson surveyed the site and named it Waterloo.

Edwin Waller, called Judge Waller, designed the city in what was called "the city plan."

The Third Congress passed legislation in January 1839 to incorporate the capital site as "the City of Austin."

By autumn, Austin had the framework of an entire city. Lamar had a presidential two-story house. Congress had a boardinghouse for residences. Log buildings were built to house various offices. Residences and business log cabins were also built. Soon, Austin had 1,500 settlers.

In October 1839, the public offices and the archives were moved from Houston City to Austin. Then Lamar arrived. The settlers rejoiced at his presence. Judge Waller was elected by the citizens to receive him.

> *With pleasure, I introduce to you the citizens of Austin, and at their request give you cordial welcome to a place which owes its existence as a city to the policy of your administration. Under your appointment, and in accordance with your direction, I came here in the month of May last for the purpose of preparing proper accomodations* [sic] *for the transaction of the business of the government. I found a situation naturally most beautiful, but requiring much exertion to render it available for the purpose in tended by its location.*

Judge Waller recalled a supply chain issue and a medically induced worker shortage. He was most concerned about the attacks from the Native Americans. He contributed the attacks to the Anglo progress in the area.

> *Building materials and provisions were to be procured, when both were scarce; a large number of workmen were to be employed in the lower country and brought up in the heat of summer, during the season when fever was rife; and when here, our labors were liable every moment to be interrupted by the hostile Indians, for whom we were obliged to be constantly on the watch; many-tongued rumor was busy with tales of Indian depredations, which seemed to increase in geometrical progression to her progress through the country.*

That said, the attacks were overblown in Judge Waller's estimation. The stories of them were fueled by those who didn't want the capital to be in Austin. He said that many settlers were able to overlook the issue in order to live in a metropolis filled with natural beauty.

Left: Edwin Waller. *Courtesy of the Texas State Library and Archives Commission.*

Below: An architectural plan for the city of Austin, circa 1840, that shows the President's House on the right, Capitol Hill at the end and Bullock's Tavern on the left. *Bill Malone Photography, courtesy of the Portal to Texas History.*

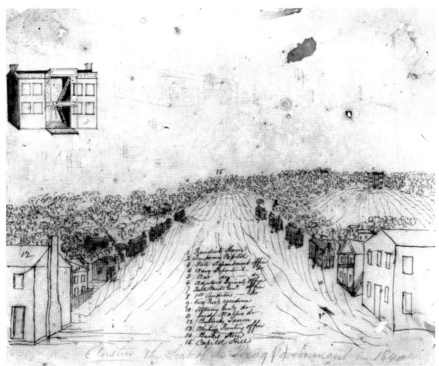

Beauty of scenery, centrality of location and purity of atmosphere have been nothing in the vision of those whose views were governed by their purses, and whose ideas of fitness were entirely subservient to their desire for profit. Under all these disadvantageous circumstances, and more which I can not [sic] now detail, a capitol, a house for the chief magistrate of the republic, and a large number of public offices were to be erected and in readiness for use in the short period of four months.

Not discouraged at the unpromising aspect of affairs, I cheerfully undertook to obey your behests. Numbers of the present citizens of Austin immigrated hither, and with an alacrity and spirit of accommodation, for which they have my grateful remembrance, rendered us every assistance in their power. To the utmost extent of my abilities I have exerted myself and have succeeded in preparing such accommodations as I sincerely hope will prove satisfactory to your excellency and my fellow citizens of Texas.

In the name of the citizens of Austin, I cordially welcome you and your cabinet to the new metropolis.

THE WALLER WALLOP

The movement of the capital to Austin was more than a political divide. It was a culmination of hotly contested visions for Texas that began during the revolution. Anglo men had created movements for Texas futures that looked nothing alike.

The battle for the capital was rooted in the divide over where leadership should locate the center of Texas economic progress. Lamar wanted what could be called an intermodal station in Austin to support interior locations and western territories that still needed to be developed.

Houston wanted the capital on the gulf, where ships and boats could do business through established routes and waterways with already established communities.

By the time the Third Congress arrived, these factions were continuing their fights at the capital of the Republic of Texas.

Waller was an original Wharton Party member from the moment Houston stated he opposed war to secure independence from Mexico (although Houston obviously later changed that stance).

Waller stumped for his friend Lamar. He also supported the war movement that included Huston and Sherman.

For that loyalty, Lamar nominated him before the capital move as the postmaster general in December 1839. Houston and his supporters deeply opposed the nomination.

As was the custom for Houston, he and his faction sought an opponent. They nominated Albert C. Horton of Matagorda.

Like the election of 1838, Houston's faction began a bitter political attack on Waller. During the campaign, they launched an attack on the floor of the house, and Waller became angry.

Waller had heard from a political ally that the entire attack was orchestrated solely by Horton. He confronted the opponent, but Horton denied it.

In response, Waller rushed him and started a fight on the house floor in front of Lamar. Horton, being larger and stronger, began to easily beat Waller.

The entire congress began screaming and hollering, which upset the president. Lamar began ordering, "Part them—separate the combatants!" But no one listened. Congressional members later described their conduct as the "act of observing in attentive neutrality."

Waller, as he recalled the story later, had greater intelligence and "wit" than Horton. He soon began to take control of the fight. When he began winning, Waller recalled, Lamar changed his orders. He told Congress, "Do not interrupt them, let them fight, let them arrange it without interference."

By the time the rumors of the fight reached the townspeople, Waller's former employees had also heard. They feared "that the congress was murdering, maiming, or hanging their old 'boss.'"

Everyone rushed to the capitol building. In the chaos that ensued, the townspeople separated the two and stopped the fight.

Waller, flushed and weary, recalled that he tried to calm the mortified townspeople, even as he was "bleeding from every vein." He said they wanted to attack Horton for the vicious beating.

Eventually, congress had to pacify the townspeople who refused to leave. Congressional leaders from both houses tried to convince the townspeople all was well. It didn't work. The residents remained angry at the way the government behaved.

They said they wanted to know why they shouldn't burn the entire capitol over the nonsense, Waller recalled. When they did leave, each person left with disgust for every member of congress.

Then the vote for postmaster general was taken. The president of the senate, Anson Jones, cast a tie-breaking vote for Waller.

With that, Waller recalled that he shook hands with Horton. They became friends. Waller resigned the day after his confirmation. The following month, he became the first mayor of Austin.

11

MATILDA

As promised, Lamar completely reversed course on relations with the Native Americans, and it didn't take long for him to start a war.

Throughout the early years of the Texas Republic, incidents of murder, gun violence and atrocities between Anglo-Texans and the Native Americans grew in intensity.

Houston's vision that Texas could work and live peacefully among the Native Americans had been rooted in his own personal experience.

His reason for building relationships, especially with the Cherokee and Comanches, might have been up for debate, but it was always clear that he did not seek to exterminate the Native Americans.

Instead, Houston as president had worked with the Texas-based chiefs to create a large reservation on the east side of the Colorado River. Congress voided it, despite Houston's intense arguments. The Texas Senate also never ratified the treaty he had negotiated with a band of Comanches.

Houston also sought a peace boundary between the Comanche Territory and Texas. Congress refused to adhere to one Comanche requirement, and the deal fell through. When Houston left office, the Native Americans in Texas rapidly lost faith in the new republic.

Lamar considered Houston's policy with the Native Americans a disaster. Within six months of moving the capital from Houston City to Austin, he waged a series of wars on them. He ignited a firestorm that would not be extinguished until the Native Americans were forced out of Texas.

Treaty of Peace, a painting by John O. Meusebac and a colonist with the Comanches. It depicts an attempted peace treaty with Native Americans. *Courtesy of Mrs. Ernest Marschull and Texas State Library and the Archives Commission.*

Austin was located on the border of the western Native American territory and was previously home to a band of Comanches. Lamar believed that as Austin grew, hostilities with Native Americans would grow, too.

Unlike Houston, he also believed that peaceful assimilation or a separate-but-equal existence would never occur. His platform had overwhelming Anglo support on both sides of the Colorado River.

One of Lamar's first acts was to sign two bills in December 1838 that would form regiments and volunteers to protect the north and west frontiers. The eight volunteer companies would serve six-month deployments in hostile territories.

A few months later, in February 1839, Lamar made the call for volunteers to protect the west.

> *I am forced by the suffering conditions of our North Western* [sic] *frontier, to make an appeal to your valor and patriotism, which have never been appealed to in vain* [sic]. *The fierce and perfidious savages are waging upon our exposed and defenceless* [sic] *inhabitants, an unprovoked and cruel warfare, masacreing* [sic] *the women and children, and threatning* [sic] *the whole line of our unprotected borders with speedy desolation.*

All that a brave and energetic people could achieve for their own safety has been nobly done. They have met their enemies with unflinching hearts, and have borne their trials and reverses with a fortitude equaled only by their heroism. But their population, thinned by repeated and continued losses, are no longer able to sustain themselves against the overwhelming numbers by which they are surrounded; and if immediate relief be not intended, they will be compelled to break up their settlements, and seek security in our more populous counties.

In May 1839, Lamar learned that Mexico had rejuvenated its plans to enlist Native Americans as mercenaries in a war against the Anglo settlers. This revelation was no surprise to him.

It justified Lamar's plans to end a disaster he believed Houston was not prepared to handle.

THE CHEROKEE WAR

During Lamar's term, he forced Native Americans out of Texas with a show of force. The Caddo, Shawnee, Kickapoo, Delaware and others all accepted armed escorts during their exit from the republic. He expected the Cherokees to follow suit.

In 1839, he appointed Kelsy H. Douglass to command the removal of the Cherokees. Burleson, Rusk and Willis H. Landrum helped him. They moved the Cherokees into Arkansas.

The Cherokees in Texas were neutral during the revolution and had a good relationship with Houston. About three hundred Cherokees arrived in Texas in the early 1800s via Arkansas.

In the 1820s, Chief Bowl brought about sixty Cherokee families into Texas to live along the Trinity River. They were villagers who were friends with the Caddos, who had been mercenaries for Mexico.

In 1835, when the Texan rebellion was starting, a concern that the Cherokees might join forces with Mexico was rising. To quell this concern, Houston negotiated a truce.

It was not his first time working with the Cherokees. Houston was a Cherokee citizen. The tribe's members called him by two names "Raven" and "Big Drunk." The first time he lived with them, he was a runaway teen. He lived among them as an act of rebellion.

Left: A portrait of Sequoyah, a Cherokee, depicts the ways Cherokee incorporated European dress and technologies *Charles Bird King, author's collection; from the public domain.*

Below: A group of Comanche watch on as a caravan travels through a Trans-Pecos valley in West Texas. *Arthur Tracey Lee, courtesy of Witte Museum.*

That experience changed him forever. He immersed himself in every aspect of Cherokee life. He wore Cherokee clothes and respected their governance, language, culture and educational system.

Cherokee chief Oolooteka was an adopted father to him. The chief assured him he would always have a home with the Cherokees.

Throughout his life, Houston would leave and reenter Native American worlds as a Cherokee citizen. At one point, he married a Cherokee woman, Diana or Tiana, according to Cherokee law. It didn't matter that he was already legally married in the United States to Eliza, a Tennessee woman. He would eventually leave his marriages to both women.

Despite the Cherokees' ability to war with Anglo settlers, they were interested in European settlers and adopted many of their technological advancements and lifestyle trends. They had adopted many of their ways. The idea that they would allow Houston to marry a Cherokee was not inconceivable.

While the merits and goals of Houston's decisions during his two terms as a Republic of Texas president remain a source of debate, he was a Native American advocate at a time when most Anglos in Texas and the United States considered Native Americans to be nothing but savages.

Lamar had a plan to end Houston's advocacy approach. Between May and December 1839, he attempted to execute a removal treaty. The Cherokees agreed to leave if they could do so without armed military escorts. This requirement stalled negotiations.

In response, the Texans marched on Cherokee villages. When the Cherokees ran, the troops followed and marched on the villages or hideouts where they sought refuge.

Hundreds of Cherokees were killed in different skirmishes and battles. The campaign ended when Burleson stopped the Cherokees from skirting along Anglo settlements to reach Mexico. In that final battle, important Cherokee leaders were killed.

After that, Texas had no more incidents with the Cherokees.

THE COUNCIL HOUSE FIGHT

The Comanches, however, were not so easily handled.

In the spring of 1840, a band of Comanches sought peace and protection inside the Republic of Texas. The Penatekas, who lived on the outskirts of

Austin, hoped to find refuge from the Cheyennes and Arapahos who battled against them in the north Comanche Territory.

Penatekas were also known as "honey eaters" and were one of at least twelve bands that comprised the Comanche Nation.

It was this band of Comanches whom Houston had negotiated a treaty with that was never ratified.

An important point about Comanche governance during this period was the lack of a central leader. The members had a fluid approach to rules and membership. This approach spread through all the different bands. Bands acted like "family groups" rather than a "group of citizens."

Each band handled its own affairs with cooperation from other bands. Temporary chiefs assumed leadership on projects that involved more than one band. Once the project ended, the temporary chief relinquished leadership.

The Comanche name is derived from the Ute word for "anyone who fights me all the time," which could also be interpreted as "enemy."

Spaniards applied the word to them when the Comanches moved into the plains. Comanches, however, knew themselves as Nermernuh, or "the people."

The Penatekas were the southernmost Comanche band. Some accounts state they settled in Texas in the 1740s. They lived east of the Pecos River, west of the Colorado River and north of the headwaters of the Central Texas rivers.

For their March 19, 1840 meeting with the Republic of Texas negotiators, they brought thirty-three chiefs and warriors to the Council House in San Antonio. Thirty-two other Comanche members accompanied them.

A main condition for Texas was the release of all the Texas prisoners that the Comanches had in custody. Texas had expected to see all the prisoners at the meeting.

Instead, the band arrived with a few Mexicans and an Anglo settler named Matilda Lockhart. Matilda was about thirteen years old when she and her sister were captured two years earlier. She had burn scars and a mutilated nose.

Her physical state convinced the Texans to believe her when she said her captors had physically and sexually abused her. She said they especially enjoyed waking her up by burning her nose.

When she told the Texans that the Comanche Nation still held thirteen other Anglo-Texans in captivity for ransom, the Texans demanded the captives be released.

The chief in charge of the delegation, Muguara, explained he had no authority over the other bands that had captured Texans.

The Texans did not believe him and soon ordered the military to flood the Council House.

The troops took all the chiefs as prisoners. They refused to release them until the Comanches released all the captive Texans.

Hearing that statement, the chiefs tried to escape and called for the delegation to help them. A violent skirmish started. Six or seven Texans were killed. Between eight and twenty others were wounded.

Thirty Penatekas were killed, including five women and children, but the chiefs escaped.

Texas captured twenty-seven Comanches and freed one woman. They told her to tell the Comanches the Penatekas would be released when the Texas captives were freed.

The Council House Fight was a disaster that started a Comanche Nation retaliatory raid against Texas. The Penatekas saw the Council House event as a bitter betrayal from the Republic of Texas. They believed the negotiation was a sanctuary of peace and that they would be free from any violence or attack during it.

The Comanches banded together when they heard about the Council House Fight. Their first move was to end all discussions about a hostage exchange.

The bands slow roasted, tortured and killed thirteen of the sixteen hostages they had. Matilda's sister was among them. The other three captives had been adopted into the bands. They lived.

THE GREAT RAID

The response to the Council House Fight did not end there. Penatekas chief Buffalo Hump sent word to the other Comanche bands to begin raiding Texas settlements.

He began his campaign with at least four hundred warriors in the Great Raid. It became one of history's largest raiding advances against an Anglo government.

Buffalo Hump started with settlements between Bastrop and San Antonio. In July, his raid expanded when every Comanche band brought a division to Texas.

An 1879 photograph of Commanche chief Buffalo Hump and his favorite wives. *L.A. Huffman, courtesy of the Montanta Historical Research Center.*

About one thousand warriors arrived from bands such as the Nokoni, Kotsoteka, Yamparika and Kwahadi.

They had no overall set of rules. Coming out of West Texas, they roamed in large bands, burning and plundering towns. When they chose to kill Anglo settlers, they did so in whatever method they desired.

The Great Raid arrived in full force in August 1840, when about six hundred Comanche warriors startled Victoria residents. The warriors rode throughout town and killed dozens of residents.

Settler and business owner John J. Linn said that the warriors even killed the enslaved men who were working in the fields. Of the twenty-five people who were slain, eight were Black and one was Mexican. The Native Americans left when the residents returned gunfire.

Residents claimed one thousand warriors (historians believe it was about five hundred Comanche) arrived in Linnville near Port Lavaca later that month. It was a prosperous place on the trade route between New Orleans and San Antonio.

The settlers' account state they eventually realized the Comanches did not know much about naval warfare. The townspeople escaped by boat and watched the warriors burn, pillage and ransack the town for an entire day.

An Indian Raid.

Opposite:
A sketch
depicting an
"Indian raid"
found in an
early Texas
schoolbook.
*Author's collection;
from the public
domain.*

Right: *Comanches
of West Texas
in War Regalia*
(1830s), by
Lino Sánchez y
Tapia. *Courtesy
of the Gilcrease
Museum (Tulsa,
OK).*

Below: A
photograph of
the painting of
the Battle of
Plum Creek by
Lee Herring.
*Author's collection;
from the public
domain.*

Comanches.

Comanches du Texas Occidental: *vêtement lorsqu'ils vont à la guerre.*

The Comanches herded large numbers of cattle into pens and slaughtered them. Linnville no longer exists, but when it did, settlers valued the town goods at $300,000.

Linn noted that his warehouse had several cases of hats and umbrellas belonging to James Robinson, a San Antonio merchant. They were destroyed after the Comanches played with them. He described the mayhem like it was a riot.

> *These the Indians made free with, and went dashing about the blazing village, amid their screeching squaws and "little Injuns," like demons in a drunken saturnalia, with Robinson's hats on their heads and Robinson's umbrellas bobbing about on every side like tipsy young balloons.*

He noted that the warriors took captives and stole livestock.

> *After loading the plunder onto pack mules, the raiders, attired in their booty, finally retired in the afternoon with some 3,000 horses and a number of captives, including Mrs. Watts, and encamped across the bayou near the old road.*

After Linnville, the Comanches headed north. At Plum Creek, on August 11, 1840, they found Felix Huston, along with Burleson and the Texas Rangers under the command of Ben McCulloch.

The Texans killed fifty Comanches.

Houston was wrong. Lamar was right. Peace did not come.

Matilda, the child at the Council House Fight, did not find peace either. She never held her head up again. Her injuries never healed. Instead of finding a new life, she died within thirty-six months after her release from the Penatekas.

12

TRUTH IN THE CAPITAL

W hen Lamar could not run for a consecutive term, Houston came back for the presidency with gusto.

Houston began his second term after a campaign that was as bitter but less bizarre than the one he organized in 1838. This time, he campaigned against Burnet, who wanted to keep Lamar's vision of a Texas empire alive.

Houston Displayed again took center stage when Burnet supporters republished it. Then a new political smear campaign emerged. A series of anonymous op-ed pieces began appearing signed with the name "Publius."

As with Coleman's pamphlet, everyone knew the author. It was Burnet. Under the penname, he wrote sixty-six vicious columns that attacked Houston.

In response, Houston began attacking "Publius" with a series of op-eds signed "Truth," in which he particularly liked to call Burnet a "Hog Thief."

Sometimes, Houston would call Burnet "King Wetumka," which meant "hog thief" in a Native American language, probably Cherokee.

Although Houston also used a penname, everyone knew it was Houston who was slurring Burnet's name.

The nasty op-eds captured public attention. James Morgan, who commanded Galveston during the revolution and sailed refugees to the island, was a spectator with a strong opinion. In January 1841, he wrote to a friend:

> *We have a bad state of affairs here now.—Lamar, the poor imbecile, could not hold out and had to give up the helm of state to Burnet, who is even*

more worthless.…Old Sam H. with all his faults appears to be the only man for Texas. He is still unsteady, intemperate, but drunk in a ditch is worth a thousand of Lamar and Burnet.…Burnet has rendered himself supremely ridiculous is so much disliked and being naturally of turbulent disposition that he has become as snarlish as a half-starved dog dealing forth anathemas against everybody.…[R]eport says he challenged Gen. Houston because H. intimated that B. was a hog thief.

Indeed, the slight might have triggered Burnet, because he did challenge Houston to a duel. He sent Branch T. Archer to issue it. Houston laughed it off. He told Archer that Burnet would have to get in line, as dozens of people wanted the chance to kill him. Besides, he replied, he was sure everyone was sick of them both.

Burnet's vitriol made it easy for Houston to gain favor with the voters. He responded in a snarky style sprinkled with his brand of grand storytelling.

"Truth" featured a character named Grog, who was sometimes unsteady on his feet. One of Grog's regular escapades included stumbling around Texas, telling lies and declaring that many people on his path were drunk. Houston wrote in one column:

> [Y]*ou swelled to a most consequential degree; and really the collar of your shirt, from connection to your imagination, I presume outtopped your ears, while your step was as lofty and aimless too, as that of a blind horse! Was there any liquor in this? It appeared so to those who dared to question the indomitable sobriety of the illustrious hero, Davy G. Burnet.*

Then Houston charged Burnet with swindling hundreds of settlers out of their life savings.

> *You prate about the faults of other men, while the blot of foul unmitigated treason rests upon you. You political brawler and canting hypocrite, whom the waters of Jordan could never cleanse from your political and moral leprosy.*

Newspapers jumped into the fray and took sides. The *Texas Sentinel* proclaimed that Houston would regularly "blaspheme his God by the most horrible oaths that ever fell from the lips of man."

The pro-Houston paper, *Houston Morning Sun*, captured the weariness the political fights had on the settlers. The paper's editor wrote, "We should be heartily glad when this political canvas is over."

Whether Houston was stupidly drunk or not, the voters tossed their support back to the hero of San Jacinto. Houston garnered 7,508 votes, a landslide against Burnet's 2,574. At the inauguration, reports circulated that Houston had not drunk a drop of any refreshing adult beverage.

Where Lamar reversed everything Houston had done, Houston began to reverse everything Lamar had done.

Houston would dismantle Lamar's Texas Empire vision. He dispatched a minister to Washington to open negotiations for the annexation of Texas.

Lamar had sent the navy to assist with a revolt in the Yucatan. Houston recalled the navy. Then he sold every ship and shuttered the naval forces in the republic.

Regarding the demands from the army, Huston proposed a final campaign to capture Matamoros. Houston, who was never enthusiastic about any port takeover, nixed the plan.

The list went on, but the only proposal that caused citizens to wage war with him was the time he tried to return the capital to Houston City.

ARCHIVE TEMPERS

Austin didn't officially become the capital under Lamar when he arrived on October 17, 1839. Austin became the capital when the archives arrived in the General Land Office on October 14, 1839. Their arrival was enough to open the capital for business.

The president didn't even need to be there.

Archives record the transactions, decisions and history of a government. They are the records of what a government has done.

Historian Dorman H. Winfrey noted that the trove of pre-republic archives included "all the land titles, the treaties between Texas and the European powers, the tattered banners and trophies of the battle of San Jacinto, the seal of the Republic, the military records of the revolutionary period, and miscellaneous manuscripts and documents comprising the official papers of the government."

In essence, a capital might move, but a government moves with the archives.

The rebel government under Burnet knew this. They loaded the archives into saddlebags and trunks when the revolution began. They guarded them and traveled with them wherever the government went. If Mexico had ever taken control of the archives, the revolution would have ended right there.

One might say that Houston fought Santa Anna on the battlefield while Burnet guarded the archives from Santa Anna.

When congress moved the archives from Columbia to Houston, they were loaded into trunks. Stephen F. Austin had the task of organizing them. He died before he could complete the job.

Between August and October 1839, John P. Borden, the first land office commissioner, used about fifty wagons to move the archives between Houston City and Austin at the cost of $6,215.

When the archives arrived in Austin, the moment held gravitas for the residents. Housing the archives in the General Land Office meant the government seat was permanent. It didn't matter who was president.

When Houston's campaign started, he criticized the capital move, because Austin sat next to Native American settlements. It was a legitimate critique.

For decades, Austin settlers lived with daily threats from the Native Americans who wandered the capital, recalled J.K. Holland in 1898.

> *The war-cry of the Indians could be heard in the night-time* [sic] *within the very gates of the capital. It was not safe for any man to go alone or without his gun beyond the limits of the town; for there was great danger of being shot or captured by the redskins who lay waiting in the mountains around for an opportunity to steal, rob, or murder.*

The Comanche presence near Austin wore on Houston's mind. Although he and his supporters believed that the future of Texas was on the coast, he was also concerned that the Comanches would attack the capital.

He even wrote to his fiancée, Anna Ragout, that the Comanches had proved they could burn the town, destroy the archives and murder the townspeople.

Other civic leaders along the Texas coast also believed that the archives were in peril in Austin. The *Houston Morning Star* wrote an editorial that stated, "[A]ll communications between it [Austin] and the inhabited portions of the country are almost cut off. Let the Archives be removed to the city of Houston; three fourths of the people of Texas would acquiesce and rejoice in a removal of this kind and the present generation will reward the effort by their fervent and honest approbation."

BEAUTIFUL AUSTIN

Houston never took to Austin at all. He rarely resided in the president's quarters. Instead, Houston stayed at the establishment of a former San Felipe resident, Angelina Peyton.

One account stated that on December 15, 1841, Houston arrived in Austin to the warm welcome of the city's residents. A large group met him with the mayor. Houston replied with a dignified and elegant address, and then he was escorted to Angelina's business, Eberly House, where he had a light, informal meal.

Angelina Peyton and her first husband, Jonathan, were members of Austin's Old Three Hundred. At San Felipe de Austin, they owned many town lots. Angelina didn't just own the business that acted as the unofficial Texas Capitol.

When Jonathan died in 1834, Angelina became a single mother who supported Texas independence. According to the minutes of the consultation in November 1835, she gave her oxen and wagon to the revolutionary cause.

Once San Felipe burned, she went to Columbia. She married a widow, Captain Jacob Eberly, a veteran of the Battle of San Jacinto. They moved to Bastrop and then to Austin, where they were living in August 1840.

Angelina opened the Eberly House that same year. The following year, her second husband, Jacob Eberly, died. Like her place in San Felipe, the Eberly House became a gathering spot for community and politics.

The new capitol in Austin in 1840. *Courtesy of the Library of Congress.*

Angela and Captain Eberly probably arrived in Austin after riding rickety stagecoaches. Buggies had not begun to travel to the frontier, recalled Holland. When they did, passengers had to be prepared to help pry the buggies out of mudholes. Passengers had to carry fencer rails on their shoulders frequently.

Austin homes had no parlors. They were not gentle accommodations. They did not have the amenities of higher-class residences. Austin, like San Felipe de Austin, had been designed for function over form.

Grocers sold only liquor, and Holland remembered the town had not designated saloons. Grocers filled that void. Settlers traveled to Barton Springs and Mount Bonnell for recreation.

Eventually, Houston moved from Angelina's establishment into the President's House when Congress was in session. The rest of the time, he lived in Houston City.

13

VIGILANTES AND CIVIL UNREST

While no second Mexican invasion ever occurred, Santa Anna harassed Texas with the possibility. He wanted to make it difficult for the republic to succeed. His threats made the settlers skittish.

In the spring of 1842, warnings went into the settlements and towns that Mexico had poised itself to invade. Settlements, including Austin, were immediately deserted. Settlers fled to the east side of the Brazos River.

On March 5, 1842, seven hundred Mexican troops descended on San Antonio, where they stayed for two days before leaving.

Houston's concerns about a Comanche raid turned to the possibility of a Mexican invasion. Austin had become vulnerable.

He declared a state of emergency. On March 10, 1842, he instructed Secretary of War George W. Hockley to move the archives from Austin to Houston City.

Houston interpreted that the constitution gave him the power to protect the archives in a time of war.

The destruction of the national archives would entail irremediable injury upon the whole people of Texas, and their safe preservation should be a consideration of paramount importance to that officer of the government who is responsible for such safe preservation. The constitution of the country— the supreme law of the land—the expression of the immediate will of the people, has devolved this high and sacred obligation upon the President. Should the infinite evil which the loss of the national archives would

Land Commissioner Thomas William "Peg Leg" Ward. *Courtesy of the Austin History Center, Austin Public Library.*

occasion, fall upon the country through his neglect of imperious constitutional duty, he would be culpable in the extreme, and most justly incur the reproach of a whole nation.

Houston told Peg Leg Ward, whose real name was Thomas W. Ward, to prepare the archives for removal. (Ward received the nickname after he lost his leg during the siege in Bexar.)

Houston appointed Ward to succeed Borden as the land commissioner in honor of his war sacrifice and service.

Ward couldn't prepare the archives, however. The residents had no intention of allowing the archives to leave Austin.

The local military commander, Colonel Henry Jones, sided with the residents. The residents believed Houston was exploiting circumstances so he could move capital.

In response to his efforts to move the archives, they created a vigilance committee.

Sixty armed guards stood at the land office and watched Ward do his job. They also created a road check in Bastrop. They inspected every wagon leaving Austin to make sure the archives were not in any one of them.

Ward eventually wrote to Houston that the situation was becoming untenable for him. He wasn't afraid of the Comanches or the Mexican military killing him—he was afraid the citizens would attack him.

> *I cannot consider the Archives at all safe at this point, and should be most willing to yield the most implicit obedience to the order of the President for the removal of the archives to a place of greater safety if the means of transportation were furnished, although it should be at the risk of my personal safety.*

The residents had a deep distrust of Houston because he did not live and govern in Austin throughout the year. They decided he had abandoned the seat of government. Moving the archives was his next step to removing the capital from Austin.

One resident, John Welch, wrote Houston a fiery personal letter. He made it clear the residents would start a war over the archives. He also had charged Houston with backpedaling and denying he wanted to move the archives after he learned of the hostility toward him. (The letter is reprinted as Welch wrote it.)

> *Now Sam you told a dam lie for you did promise the people in Houston that you would move it, and I heard a man say that you told Hockley not to bring all his servants because you would all go back soon. But the truth is that you are afeard you Dam old drunk Cherokee we dont thank you becase we would shot you and every dam waggoner that you could start with the papers you cant do it and ax you no odds Travis and Bastrop Fayette Gonzales can bring 1000 Men out and Ned Burleson and Lewis P. Cook have promised that you shant budge with the papers I heard them myself and you know Burleson and Cook can make you squat you dam blackgard indian drunk.*

Within a week, Sam Whiting also wrote Lamar that the community would take up arms against Houston if he moved the archives.

In what was either a calculated move or true admiration, Houston had nothing but glowing words about the Austinites who wanted to keep the archives. He still believed, however, the control of the archives put his reputation on the line. He also believed the residents could die if they kept them.

He wrote that he appreciated the "patriotic disposition envinced [*sic*] by the citizens of Travis county to defend the national archives at the hazard of their lives, should they be permitted to remain in Austin, and entertains no doubt their pledges to this effect would be nobly redeemed, should invasion press upon them, but the hazards of war are always great; nor could the mere possession of the archives at Austin be justly considered a suitable equivalent for the loss of life which the contest might occasion—even if successful."

His response to the vigilante committee was to call a special session of congress in Houston City on June 27, 1842. He tried to convince the members to let him remove the archives.

Congress did not agree to any of Houston's proposals.

SECOND SAN ANTONIO OCCUPATION

The issue died down until September 11, 1842, when the Mexican army staged a second occupation in San Antonio with 1,400 troops. This attack had no advance warning. They used a smuggling trail to enter the city.

The second occupation was more alarming than the first. The Mexican military took several hostages who worked at the district courts. The residents surrendered after a brief skirmish.

The town was under Mexican control for one week. A military unit hunted the Mexican army through Texas for one month before they left the republic.

Austin businesses closed, and Ward shuttered the land office on September 28. Settlers, including Austinites, fled the interior of Texas.

As people left Austin, those who stayed, like Angelina, intensified their hatred of Houston.

They charged that since he had abandoned the capital months earlier, he had no idea how they felt or what they needed. He was oblivious to their reality. Many pondered that the Mexican army might move north to Austin.

The second Mexican occupation gave Houston the ammunition he needed. He renewed his attempts to move the archives.

During this time, Houston wrote in a letter that he was "certain that Mexico was planning a second invasion and the only reason troops fell from San Antonio was to regroup and join more forces on the Rio Grande."

> *It is indeed true that the immediate cause which induced the order for the removal of the archives, has for the time ceased to exist; there is no assurance that it may not be renewed in a more formidable shape at the early period.*
>
> *Austin, situated at a point remote from the sea-board and almost insulated from the whole country, eminently exposed to attack both by the Indian and Mexican foe, and liable all the time to become the very theatre of war, is deemed at this crisis by the Executive to be very unsuitable as a point for carrying on the multifarious operations of the government.*

A few weeks later, Houston called for the department offices in Austin to move to Washington-on-the-Brazos. He held the regular session of congress there on December 5, 1842.

The residents still would not let Ward move the archives, so they stayed in Austin. Congress still did not agree with Houston. They did not approve of an executive resolution Houston had made to force their hand.

THE BLUE NORTHERNER

Congress and the vigilante committee did not stop Houston.

Five days later, a covert operation to remove the archives began.

Houston gave Colonel Thomas I. Smith and Captain Eli Chandler complete authority to perform the mission however they chose. In his instructions, Houston wrote:

> *It would, also, be well to conduct your operations with the utmost secrecy; and by all means raise a sufficient force to take possession of and guard the archives, before any rumor of your intended visit could possibly be received there. You might raise your men as if for an Indian excursion; and by no means let your object be known till you are ready to act. Threats have been made, that if the Archives are ever removed, they will be in ashes. The loss to the country would be infinite and irreparable.*

A blue northerner blew into Austin on December 30, 1842. This was the same day the operatives arrived with twenty troops and three wagons. Ward opened the door, and the men began working.

Another land office employee, George Durham, was staunchly opposed to the operation. He held firm that the papers should not be given to the men. Smith and Chandler said they were acting under Houston's orders.

It was about midnight when Angelina Eberly finished for the evening at the Eberly House. She saw a wagon being loaded in the alley behind the land office. She understood what she was seeing.

Since the evacuation, Austin had only about ten armed men, so she and the townspeople let the covert operation continue. They gathered about fifty men from surrounding settlements.

The next day, a sizable but poorly armed crowd was in Austin. They walked with Angelina to Congress Avenue, where Lamar had earlier placed a loaded six-pound howitzer. He intended for the community to use it against the Comanches. Instead, they used it against Houston's men.

The group turned the muzzle on the land office, Angelina lit the torch and the cannon fired.

It was noon when Ward heard the town's response.

> *Much excitement prevailed here, a howitzer loaded with grape was discharged at my residence after I had heard the cry of "blow the old house to pieces" eight shot perforated the buildings.*

AUSTIN ABOUT 1839 OR 1841.

Above: A photograph of a print depicting Austin directly before or after the Texas Archive War. It is found in the book *Austin Yesterday and Today*. *Courtesy of the Portal to Texas History*

Opposite: A sketch from an 1875 Texas scrapbook depicts Angelina Eberly firing the cannon at Houston's team as they try to steal the Republic of Texas Archives. *Author's collection; from the public domain.*

The grape shot did not hurt anyone, but it did interrupt the operation, and it damaged the building. Houston's men left with what they had.

Ward sent two of his employees to guard the archives, since no one knew where they were going. Houston's men moved the archives into trunks pulled by oxen. They used Caldwell Road to circumvent the roadblock in Bastrop. Meanwhile, the community loaded the cannon and began following them on foot.

Houston's men made it about eighteen miles north of Austin at Kenney's Fort. The blue northerner was in full force, and the weather became bitterly cold. The men picketed themselves with cedar posts, but they did not stand guard.

At some point between the depths of night and the dawn of the morning, they found themselves surrounded by the townspeople.

The Austinites gave Smith a choice to surrender the archives or face them. He surrendered the archives. It was either a dramatic scene or an anticlimactic one, depending on who told the story.

The townspeople drove the oxen back to Austin with Houston's men. When they arrived on December 31, the Austin women prepared a dinner.

It's unclear if Houston's men attended, but the townspeople enjoyed a night of celebration.

They took the archives to Angelina's home, where armed guards stood over them. Angelina always supported the vigilante committee against Houston.

He was the man who tried to steal the archives from the capital she rose to defend.

He was also the man who burned San Felipe de Austin, the town where all she loved had been.

14

AUSTIN FOREVERMORE

Houston never returned to Austin. He governed from Washington-on-the-Brazos until he left office. Congress met there in session.

He had the seals brought to him. Ward built a new land office that housed the new archives congress created.

Houston eventually realized the residents would not ever let the archives leave Angelina's custody. He acquiesced and agreed to let her and the settlers keep them.

He never dispatched armed guards or the military to demand their return.

Holland remembered the time the government operated at Washington-on-the-Brazo. The accommodation was worse than those they had in Houston City.

The government had to rent the gambling hall above the town's largest saloon. It was remodeled for the house of representatives to "protect them from temptation."

> *Washington was a small village, and it was difficult for the government to obtain suitable rooms for Congress. About the biggest building in the town was Hatfield's "grocery," or saloon as we now say; but that was a very important place of resort, where congressmen and strangers were most in the habit of congregating. It was in fact too important a place to give up for other purposes; but it was finally yielded to the House of Representatives.*

THE INVESTIGATION

Within a matter of months, congress convened a house committee to investigate Houston and his operation. They called it the Archive Committee.

The committee delivered their report on January 16, 1843. On that date, Angelina still had guards standing over the archives at her house.

The committee declared the entire operation could have gone horribly wrong. If one thing had gone differently, Texas could have had a civil war.

> *The intelligence laid before the House by the Executive, exhibits the startling fact that the country has but just escaped the horrors of a civil war; that citizens has been armed against citizen and brother against brother, under the auspices of the Executive.... [T]he Congress was in session, peaceably discharging their important duties, and in ignorance of the fearful danger which overhung and threatened the country. That such a state of things should ever exist, would be much lamented, but that it should have been excited in the present emergency when the Government is striving by war to maintain its existence, and at the very time when a patriot band of our countrymen are gallantly battling in the enemy's country, in defence [sic] of the national cause, amid in vindication of national honor, is to be deprecated as the most calamitous of evils, which could threaten or befall us. What has given rise to this state of things, demands the solemn investigation of the Representatives of the people.*

The committee charged that Houston knew he had no power to remove the archives. He knew that because he had asked them for their permission, and they did not give it.

For years afterward, Houston's supporters continued to argue that he did have this power. They claimed the constitution allowed him to remove the archives in a time of war or great emergency. A Mexican occupation, they said, is an emergency.

The committee also noted that the day after Congress adjourned in Austin, Houston left and stated he would never return.

Interestingly, the committee also agreed with the Austinites about Houston. The president was so tenacious and determined to move the capital, he set the republic to plunge toward a civil war.

As an example, the committee noted that when Houston received the report that Mexico was going to advance the first time, he did nothing. He did not return to the capital to defend it or even launch a defense for San Antonio.

They called his lack of action "an insult of violated national honor."

Later, they charged that he had continued ignoring Austin while he was in Galveston. When he was there, he told residents there was no emergency. The intruders where a marauding party and not a Mexican army invasion. He told them there was no reason to defend the west.

The Archive Committee was also clear that the residents were wrong. The citizens were supposed to follow the president's order and let the archives be taken. Yet the Archive Committee extended sympathy for their actions.

> [B]*ut knowing all the circumstances as well as they did and the moving causes that actuated the Executive, it would be hard to censure them for their resistance.*

RES GASTAE

The most important charge levied against Houston was the one of res gastae. The committee believed that Houston's actions and statements were so grievous that they fell under the res gestae rule. This rule still stands today. It essentially means that Houston had conducted a criminal act when he ordered the archives' removal.

The committee believed Houston's conduct and statements made during that effort rose to the level of court evidence. In their investigation, the committee noted that the Mexicans, whether they were an army or a gang, left San Antonio before Houston issued the removal of the archives.

They also noted that Hockley, Houston's representative in Austin, would not move on the order. He told Austinites that he believed the archives were safe in that city.

In another example, the committee noted that Austin residents traveled to Houston City to meet with the president. They wanted to tell him that they did not feel Mexico would attempt to steal the archives. After they did this, Houston still refused to change the order.

Houston told the Austinites that if the archives were in Austin, Santa Anna would try to steal them from there instead of meeting him at the seaport. The house committee was blunt in their assessment of that meeting.

> *This statement if it means anything shows that his anxiety for the removal of the archives, did not arise from his conviction of their danger in Austin but for the sake of his personal convenience....Let the ignominy rest where it should.*

Sculpted by David Adickes, this sixty-seven-foot-tall statue of Sam Houston, titled *A Tribute to Courage*, can be seen for miles along Interstate 45 in Huntsville. *Dreanna L. Belden, courtesy of the Portal to Texas History.*

Later, the committee turned their attention to the orders given to Smith and Chandler. The committee charged the two had no official government role known to congress.

They noted that the men were told to remove the archives because they were on an "Indian expedition." Their orders did not include any mention of Mexican invasions. The covert and secretive nature of their orders were clearly stated in the report.

After the submission of the report, a motion was made to reject it. It passed 19–18.

The Texas Archive Wars had deeply divided the government.

The report went into the archives. Nothing happened to Houston except that a committee wrote a scathing account of him. Nothing happened to the residents.

In fact, Angelina kept the archives.

AFTERMATH

Austin became a shell of its former self when the Texas Archive War reached its height. Those who fled because of the Mexican threat appear to have stayed away. In a letter to Lamar, James Webb wrote:

> *Poor Austin has sadly changed since you saw it, as indeed, has all the Western part of the Country—We have now but a small population,—no business,—& are living under great privations—We have however, held on to the "Archives," & will battle for them to the death.*

Another reason the town languished may have been that business and economic progress throughout Texas was deeply affected the entire time Angelina kept the archives.

In 1843, republic business came to a standstill. Only six patents were issued, as none of the surveyors or draftsmen could do their jobs. Another reason people did not return might have been due to Austin's unsure future as the capital.

The republic would continue to govern itself in this state until Houston left office. Business would not flourish again until Texas was annexed into the United States.

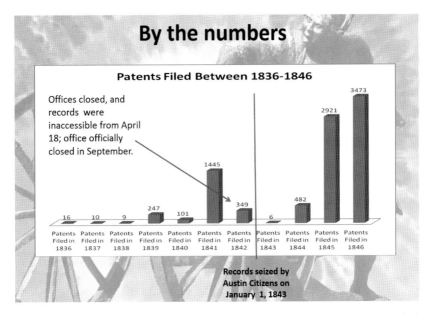

An analysis of the GLO Land Grant Database shows an extreme drop in business during the Mexican invasion of San Antonio and the Archives War. *Courtesy of the General Land Commission Office.*

A Daughters of the Republic of Texas Centennial map shows the growth of Texas through 1936. *Courtesy of the Portal of Texas History.*

A statue of Angelina Eberly in Austin, erected in 2014, depicts the moment she lit the cannon that started the Texas Archive War. *Mitchell Hobbs, author's Collection; from the public domain.*

When Anson Jones became president on December 9, 1844, the discussions Houston started with the United States to annex Texas were almost finished. In a matter of weeks, the United States approved a resolution to annex the republic.

That summer, on July 14, 1844, the Texas legislature convened to discuss the matter.

Jones called the meeting in Austin.

When he arrived, Houston and congress delivered the archives they created at Washington-on-the-Brazos.

Then the Austinites delivered the Texas archives. They never disbanded the vigilante committee. They never relinquished the pledge to guard the archives with their lives.

The day Angelina let the archives leave her house, the Texas Archives War ended.

The feud that defined the battle over the Texas capital was finished.

Austin became the seat of the Texas government forevermore.

"APOLOGY"

I NEVER hoped in life to claim
A passport to exalted fame;
'Tis not for this I sometimes frame
The simple song—
Contented still, with humble name,
To move along.

I write because there's joy in rhyme;
It cheers an evening's idle time;
And though my verse the true sublime
May never reach,
Yet Heaven will never call it crime,
If truth it teach.

The labor steals the heart from wo;
It makes it oft with rapture glow;
And always teaches to forego
Each low desire;
Then why on those our blame bestow
Who strike the lyre?

If virtue in the song be blent,
I know no reason to repent
My hours of studious content,
And lettered joy;
'Twere well if leisure ne'er was spent
In worse employ.

—Mirabeau Lamar

BIBLIOGRAPHY

Books

Brown, John Henry. *History of Texas, 1685–1892*. St. Louis, MO: L.E. Daniel, 1892.

——. *Indian Wars and Pioneers of Texas*. Austin, TX: L.E. Daniel, 1890. https://www.loc.gov/item/03014078/.

Castañeda, Carlos Eduardo. *The Mexican Side of the Texas Revolution, 1836: By the Chief Mexican Participants*. Translated with notes by C.E. Castañeda. New York: Arno Press, 1976.

Coleman, Robert M., and John Holmes Jenkins. *Houston Displayed: Or, Who Won the Battle of San Jacinto?* San Franscisco, CA: Brick Row Book Shop, 1964.

Crane, William Carey. *Life and Select Literary Remains of Sam Houston of Texas*. United States: J.B. Lippincott & Company, 1884.

Hoff, Blanche. *San Felipe de Austin; Capital of Austin's Colony*. Washington, TX: Star of the Republic Museum, 1938.

Houston, Sam, Amelia W. Williams and Eugene Campbell Barker. *The Writings of Sam Houston*. Austin: University of Texas Press, 1938.

Lamar, Mirabeau Bonaparte. *The Papers of Mirabeau Bonaparte Lamar*. Vol. 4, part 1. Edited by Charles Adams Gulick and Winnie Allen. Austin, TX: Von Beckman-Jones, 1924.

——. *The Papers of Mirabeau Bonaparte Lamar*. Vol. 4, part 2. Edited by Charles Adams Gulick and Winnie Allen. Austin, TX: Von Beckman-Jones, 1924.

Lamar, Mirabeau Bonaparte, and Philip Graham. *The Life and Poems of Mirabeau B. Lamar*. Chapel Hill: University of North Carolina Press, 1938.

Lester, C. Edwards. *Life of Sam Houston: The Only Authentic Memoir of Him Ever Published*. Champaign: University of Illinois at Urbana-Champaign, 1855.

Smithwick, Noah. *The Evolution of a State: Or, Recollections of Old Texas Days*. Austin, TX: Gammel Book Company, 1900.

Sowell, Andrew Jackson. *History of Fort Bend County: Containing Biographical Sketches of Many Noted Characters*. Waco, TX: W.M. Morrison, 1904.

Thompson, Waddy. *Recollections of Mexico: By Waddy Thompson, Esq., Late Envoy Extraordinary and Minister Plenipotentiary of the United States, at Mexico*. New York: Wiley & Putnam, 1846.

Wharton, Clarence. *The Republic of Texas: A Brief History of Texas from the First American Colonies in 1821 to Annexation in 1846*. Austin: University of Texas, 1922.

Wooten, Dudley G. *A Complete History of Texas for Schools, Colleges, and General Use*. Dallas: Texas Historical Company, 1899.

Journals and Dissertations

Barker, Eugene C. "Descriptions of Texas by Stephen F. Austin." *Southwestern Historical Quarterly* 28, no. 2 (1924): 98–121. http://www.jstor.org/stable/30234913.

Christian, Asa Kyrus. "Mirabeau Buonaparte Lamar." Master's thesis, University of Pennsylvania, 1922.

Hogan, William Ransom. "A Social and Economic History of the Republic of Texas." PhD dissertation, University of Oklahoma, 1942.

Journals of the House of Representatives of the Seventh Congress of the Republic of Texas. Washington, TX: Thomas Johnson, 1843

Kemp, L.W. "Mrs. Angelina B. Eberly." *Southwestern Historical Quarterly* 36, no. 3 (1933): 193–99. http://www.jstor.org/stable/30235443.

Kingston, Mike. "The Capitals of Texas." *Texas Almanac* (2021). https://www.texasalmanac.com/articles/the-capitals-of-texas#:~:text=15%2C%201836%2C%20ordered%20the%20seat,by%20the%20Texas%20Congress%20Jan.

Kuykendall, J.H. "Reminiscences of Early Texans: A Collection from the Austin Papers." *Quarterly of the Texas State Historical Association* 7, no. 1 (1903): 29–64. http://www.jstor.org/stable/27784946.

Labadie, N.D. "The San Jacinto Campaign." *Texas Almanac* (1859): 40–64. https://texashistory.unt.edu/ark:/67531/metapth123765/.

Muir, A.F. "Algernon P. Thompson." *Southwestern Historical Quarterly* 51 (July 1947–April 1948): 143–53. https://texashistory.unt.edu/ark:/67531/metapth101119/.

Parker, Nancy Boothe. "Mirabeau B. Lamar's Texas Journal." *Southwestern Historical Quarterly* 84, no. 2 (1980): 197–220. http://www.jstor.org/stable/30238669.

Smither, Harriet. "The Archives of Texas." *American Archivist* 3, no. 3 (1940): 187–200. http://www.jstor.org/stable/40288203.

Southwick, Leslie H. "The Presidential Election of 1838: Robert Wilson." *Houston History Magazine*, n.d. https://www.houstonhistorymagazine.org/wp-content/uploads/2014/02/13.1-The-Texas-Presidential-Election-of-1838-Robert-Wilson-Leslie-H-Southwick-.pdf.

Swanlund, Charles. "Presidential Politics in the Republic of Texas." *East Texas Historical Journal* 57, no. 1 (2019): 65–79. https://scholarworks.sfasu.edu/cgi/viewcontent.cgi?article=2830&context=ethj.

Williams, Amelia. "A Critical Study of the Siege of the Alamo and of the Personnel of Its Defenders: IV. Historical Problems Relating to the Alamo." *Southwestern Historical Quarterly* 37, no. 3 (1934): 157–84. http://www.jstor.org/stable/30235477.

Winfrey, Dorman H. "Mirabeau H. Lamar and Texas Nationalism." *Southwestern Historical Quarterly* 59, no. 2 (1955): 184–205. http://www.jstor.org/stable/30235229.

———. "The Texan Archive War of 1842." *Southwestern Historical Quarterly* 64, no. 2 (1960): 171–84. http://www.jstor.org/stable/30236161.

Winkler, Ernest William, ed. *Secret Journals of the Senate of the Republic of Texas 1836–1845*. Austin, TX: Austin Printing Company, 1911.

Winters, James Washington. "An Account of the Battle of San Jacinto." *Quarterly of the Texas State Historical Association* 6, no. 2 (1902): 139–44.

POEMS, ESSAYS AND LECTURES

Dienst, Alex. "Contemporary Poetry of the Texan Revolution." *Southwestern Historical Quarterly* 21, no. 2 (1917): 156–84. http://www.jstor.org/stable/30234747.

Lamar, Mirabeau. "Mirabeau B. Lamar, Presidential Address on the Protection of the Frontier, February 28, 1839." Austin, TX, 2013.

———. *Verse Memorials*. New York: W.P. Fetridge & Company, 1857. https://docsouth.unc.edu/southlit/lamar/lamar.html.

News Articles

Fechter, Joshua. "Texas Republicans Ended a Patchwork of Local Rules They Say Hurt Business. They Also Eroded Powers of City Councils." *Texas Tribune*, June 7, 2023. https://www.texastribune.org/2023/06/07/texas-republicans-cities-local-control/.

Garcia-Buckalew, Bob. "Grappling with Racist History: Should Austin Change the Name of Lamar Boulevard?" kvue.com. July 7, 2020. https://www.kvue.com/article/news/history/austin-lamar-boulevard-racism-name-change/269-eff12add-b079-4ac0-bdb4-12565b852c8b.

Gradney, Mia. "Sam Houston Attributed Much of His Success, Savvy to His Life with Native Americans." khou.com. December 1, 2020. https://www.khou.com/article/news/history/sam-houston-a-life-influenced-by-native-americans/285-405fa0b1-f038-40ab-86e5-f6e654ac75a8#:~:text=%22At%20a%20time%20where%20a,He%20loved%20their%20educational%20system.

Holley, D.J. "Early Texans Were Used to a Life in Peril." *Houston Chronicle*, February 28, 2022. https://www.pressreader.com/usa/houston-chronicle/20220228/281608128886059.

Lomax, John Nova. "The Problem with Mirabeau Lamar." *Texas Monthly*, September 17, 2015. https://www.texasmonthly.com/the-daily-post/the-problem-with-mirabeau-lamar/.

Longview News-Journal. "Answer Line: Cherokee History a Part of East Texas." June 20, 2020. https://www.news-journal.com/features/answer_line/answer-line-cherokee-history-a-part-of-east-texas/.

Maritime Executive. "Houston's Export Levels Grow as Port Rises in U.S. Rankings." May 16, 2023. https://maritime-executive.com/article/houston-s-export-levels-grow-as-port-rises-in-u-s-rankings.

McClear, Sheila. "The Fascinating Story of the Texas Archives War of 1842." *Smithsonian*, October 9, 2018. https://www.smithsonianmag.com/history/fascinating-story-texas-archives-war-1842-180970470/.

McLeod, Gerald E. "Stephen F. Austin Is Honored with a Statue South of Angleton." *Austin Chronicle*, June 12, 2009. https://www.austinchronicle.com/columns/2009-06-12/792740/.

Websites and Databases

Alamo. "Battle of Béxar." https://www.thealamo.org/remember/importance-of-bexar.

Beazley, Julia Beazley, and Eldon Stephen Branda. "Groce, Leonard Waller." Handbook of Texas Online. https://www.tshaonline.org/handbook/entries/groce-leonard-waller.

Berlet, Sarah Groce. "Groce's Ferry." Handbook of Texas Online. https://www.tshaonline.org/handbook/entries/groces-ferry.

Charles Christopher Jackson. "San Felipe de Austin, TX." Handbook of Texas Online. https://www.tshaonline.org/handbook/entries/san-felipe-de-austin-tx.

Covington, Carolyn Callaway. "Runaway Scrape." Handbook of Texas Online. https://www.tshaonline.org/handbook/entries/runaway-scrape.

Cutrer, Thomas W. "Royall, Richard Royster." Handbook of Texas Online. https://www.tshaonline.org/handbook/entries/royall-richard-royster.

Department of Justice, Office of Justice Programs. "Res Gestae in the Texas Court of Criminal Appeals, a Method to Their Madness." https://www.ojp.gov/ncjrs/virtual-library/abstracts/res-gestae-texas-court-criminal-appeals-method-their-madness#.

Ericson, Joe E. "Collinsworth, James." Handbook of Texas Online. https://www.tshaonline.org/handbook/entries/collinsworth-james.

Gambrell, Herbert P. "Lamar, Mirabeau Buonaparte." Handbook of Texas Online. https://www.tshaonline.org/handbook/entries/lamar-mirabeau-buonaparte.

Handbook of Texas Online. "Battle of Plum Creek." https://www.tshaonline.org/handbook/entries/plum-creek-battle-of.

———. "Cherokee War." https://www.tshaonline.org/handbook/entries/cherokee-war.

———. "Matamoros Expeditions of 1836 and 1837." https://www.tshaonline.org/handbook/entries/matamoros-expeditions-of-1836-and-1837.

Hazlewood, Claudia. "Bernardo Plantation." Handbook of Texas Online. https://www.tshaonline.org/handbook/entries/bernardo-plantation.

Huntsville Pure Texas. "About the Statue." https://www.huntsvilletexas.com/163/About-the-Statue.

Kosub, D'mitri. "The Gonzales Road in the Texas Revolution." *Lost Texas Roads*, July 12, 2020. https://losttexasroads.com/gonzales-road/gonzales-road-history/the-gonzales-road-in-the-texas-revolution/.

Kreneck, Thomas H. "Houston, Sam." Handbook of Texas Online. https://www.tshaonline.org/handbook/entries/houston-sam.

Lake, Paul D. "Consultation." Handbook of Texas Online. https://www.tshaonline.org/handbook/entries/consultation.

Lipscomb, Carol A. "Comanche Indians." Handbook of Texas Online. https://www.tshaonline.org/handbook/entries/comanche-indians.

Moore, R.E. "The Texas Comanches." Texas Indians. http://www.texasindians.com/comanche.htm.

Port Houston. "Port Statistics." August 22, 2023. https://porthouston.com/about/our-port/statistics/.

Roell, Craig H. "Linnville Raid of 1840." Handbook of Texas Online. https://www.tshaonline.org/handbook/entries/linnville-raid-of-1840.

San Jacinto Museum of History. "Isaac Lafayette Hill." https://www.sanjacinto-museum.org/Library/Veteran_Bios/Bio_page/?id=413&army=Texian.

———. "Mirabeau Lamar." https://www.sanjacinto-museum.org/The_Battle/Commanders/Texian_Commanders/Mirabeau_Lamar/.

———. "Sam Houston." https://www.sanjacinto-museum.org/The_Battle/Commanders/Sam_Houston/#Pane1.

Schilz Dickson, Jodye Lynn. "Council House Fight." Handbook of Texas Online. https://www.tshaonline.org/handbook/entries/council-house-fight.

Scribner, John C.L. "Texas Military Forces Historical Sketch: Indian Fighting." Texas Military Forces Museum. https://texasmilitaryforcesmuseum.org/tnghist8.htm.

Stephen F. Austin-Munson Historical County Park. "Stephen F. Austin-Munson Historical County Park: Brazoria County, TX." https://www.brazoriacountytx.gov/departments/parks-department/stephen-f-austin-munson-historical-county-park.

Texas General Land Office. "The Other Side of the Archives War: How the Republic of Texas and the General Land Office Were Held." *Medium*, December 29, 2017. https://txglo.medium.com/the-other-side-of-the-archives-war-how-the-republic-of-texas-and-the-general-land-office-were-held-fd286e775f68.

Texas State Library and Archive Commission. "Mirabeau B. Lamar." March 16, 2015. https://www.tsl.texas.gov/exhibits/presidents/lamar/path.html#:~:text=Lamar%20had%20just%20returned%20to,Texas%20army%20as%20a%20private.

———. "Mirabeau B. Lamar: Texas Patriot and President (1798–1859)." May 20, 2016. https://www.tsl.texas.gov/lobbyexhibits/mural-lamar.

Texas Treasures. "Mirabeau B. Lamar, Presidential Address on the Protection of the Frontier, February 28, 1839." Texas State Library and Archive Commission. April 18, 2016. https://www.tsl.texas.gov/treasures/giants/lamar/lamar-frontier-1.html.

Upchurch, Alice Gray. "Lockhart, Matilda." Handbook of Texas Online. https://www.tshaonline.org/handbook/entries/lockhart-matilda.

Weiser-Alexander, Kathy. "Council House Fight in San Antonio, Texas." *Legends of America*, December 2020. https://www.legendsofamerica.com/council-house-fight-texas/.

Wikipedia. "Cherokee." https://en.wikipedia.org/w/index.php?title=Cherokee&oldid=1172249489.

———. "Comanche Wars." https://en.wikipedia.org/w/index.php?title=Comanche_Wars&oldid=1169379419.

———. "Felix Huston." https://en.wikipedia.org/w/index.php?title=Felix_Huston&oldid=1168380902.

———. "Great Raid of 1840." https://en.wikipedia.org/w/index.php?title=Great_Raid_of_1840&oldid=1165794921.

———. "James Fannin." https://en.wikipedia.org/w/index.php?title=James_Fannin&oldid=1172214359.

———. "Runaway Scrape." https://en.wikipedia.org/w/index.php?title=Runaway_Scrape&oldid=1171044850.

INDEX

V

W

ABOUT THE AUTHOR

Lora-Marie Bernard has been called one of the state's best storytellers by "Texana Reads."

During her time as a Texas-based journalist and communicator, she won numerous Associated Press awards and national press honors for her public affairs and investigative reporting. Early in her career, she earned the Robert F. Kennedy Journalism Award.

As a Washington, D.C. field correspondent, she served as an international radio commentator, journalist and photographer for the 2016 Trump presidential campaign; the 2018 Texas U.S. Senate race; the Washington, D.C. Women's March; and Hurricane Harvey.

She's written several books for The History Press, including *The Yellow Rose of Texas: The Song, The Legend & Emily D. West*; *The Counterfeit Prince of Old Texas: Swindling Slaver Monroe Edwards*; and *Lower Brazos River Canals*. She is also the coauthor of *Houston Center: Vision to Excellence* (Green Oaks Publishing).

She earned her master's degree in liberal arts extension studies from Harvard University. She earned her undergraduate degree from the Mayborn School of Journalism at the University of North Texas.

She serves as an international corporate board member for the Alumnae-i Network for Harvard Women. She also served as the vice-president for the Southeast Texas Museum Association for several years.

Visit us at
www.historypress.com